I0426252

June 2012

JOINT STRIKE FIGHTER

DOD Actions Needed to Further Enhance Restructuring and Address Affordability Risks

GAO
Accountability * Integrity * Reliability

Highlights

Highlights of GAO-12-437, a report to congressional committees

JOINT STRIKE FIGHTER

DOD Actions Needed to Further Enhance Restructuring and Address Affordability Risks

Why GAO Did This Study

The F-35 Lightning II, also known as the Joint Strike Fighter (JSF), is the Department of Defense's (DOD) most costly and ambitious aircraft acquisition, seeking to simultaneously develop and field three aircraft variants for the Air Force, Navy, Marine Corps, and eight international partners. The JSF is critical to DOD's long-term recapitalization plans to replace hundreds of legacy aircraft. Total U.S. investment is now projected at nearly $400 billion to develop and acquire 2,457 aircraft through 2037 and will require a long-term, sustained funding commitment. The JSF has been extensively restructured over the last 2 years to address relatively poor cost, schedule, and performance outcomes.

This report, prepared in response to the National Defense Authorization Act for Fiscal Year 2010, addresses (1) JSF program cost and schedule changes and affordability issues; (2) performance objectives, testing results, and technical risks; and (3) contract costs, concurrency impacts, and manufacturing. GAO's work included analyses of a wide range of program documents and interviews with defense and contractor officials.

What GAO Recommends

GAO recommends that (1) DOD analyze cost and program impacts from potentially reduced future funding levels and (2) assess the capability and challenges facing the JSF's global supply chain. DOD concurred with the second recommendation and agreed with the value of the first, but believed its annual budget efforts are sufficient. GAO maintains that more robust data is needed and could be useful to congressional deliberations.

View GAO-12-437. For more information, contact Michael J. Sullivan at (202) 512-4841 or sullivanm@gao.gov.

What GAO Found

Joint Strike Fighter restructuring continued throughout 2011 and into 2012, adding to cost and schedule. The new program baseline projects total acquisition costs of $395.7 billion, an increase of $117.2 billion (42 percent) from the prior 2007 baseline. Full rate production is now planned for 2019, a delay of 6 years from the 2007 baseline. Unit costs per aircraft have doubled since start of development in 2001. Critical dates for delivering warfighter requirements remain unsettled because of program uncertainties. While the total number of aircraft DOD plans to buy has not changed, it has for 3 straight years reduced near-term procurement quantities, deferring aircraft and costs to future years. Since 2002, the total quantity through 2017 has been reduced by three-fourths, from 1,591 to 365. Affordability is a key challenge—annual acquisition funding needs average about $12.5 billion through 2037 and life-cycle operating and support costs are estimated at $1.1 trillion. DOD has not thoroughly analyzed program impacts should funding expectations be unmet.

Overall performance in 2011 was mixed as the program achieved 6 of 11 important objectives. Developmental flight testing gained momentum and is now about 21 percent complete with the most challenging tasks still ahead. Performance of the short takeoff and vertical landing variant improved this year and its "probation" period to fix deficiencies was ended after 1 year with several fixes temporary and untested. Developing and integrating the more than 24 million lines of software code continues to be of concern. Late software releases and concurrent work on multiple software blocks have delayed testing and training. Development of critical mission systems providing core combat capabilities remains behind schedule and risky. To date, only 4 percent of the mission systems required for full capability have been verified. Deficiencies with the helmet mounted display, integral to mission systems functionality and concepts of operation, are most problematic. The autonomic logistics information system, integral technology for improving aircraft availability and lowering support costs, is not fully developed.

Most of the instability in the program has been and continues to be the result of highly concurrent development, testing, and production activities. Cost overruns on the first four annual procurement contracts total more than $1 billion and aircraft deliveries are on average more than 1 year late. Program officials said the government's share of the cost growth is $672 million; this adds about $11 million to the price of each of the 63 aircraft under those contracts. Effectively managing the expanding network of global suppliers will be key to improving program outcomes, increasing manufacturing throughput, and enabling higher production rates. In addition to contract overruns, concurrency costs of at least $373 million have been incurred on production aircraft to correct deficiencies found in testing. The manufacturing process is still absorbing higher than expected number of engineering changes resulting from flight testing, changes which are expected to persist at elevated levels into 2019, making it difficult to achieve efficient production rates. More design and manufacturing changes are expected as testing continues, bringing risks for more contract overruns and concurrency costs. Even with the substantial reductions in near-term production quantities, DOD still plans to procure 365 aircraft for $69 billion before developmental flight tests are completed.

_____ United States Government Accountability Office

Contents

Tables

Figures

Abbreviations

ALIS	Autonomic Logistics Information System
CAPE	Cost Assessment and Program Evaluation
CTOL	conventional takeoff and landing
CV	carrier variant
DCMA	Defense Contract Management Agency
DOD	Department of Defense
DOT&E	Director, Operational Test and Evaluation
DT	development testing
JSF	Joint Strike Fighter
LRIP	low rate initial production
OSD	Office of the Secretary of Defense
SDD	system development and demonstration
STOVL	short takeoff and vertical landing

GAO
Accountability * Integrity * Reliability

United States Government Accountability Office
Washington, DC 20548

June 14, 2012

Congressional Committees

The F-35 Lightning II, also known as the Joint Strike Fighter (JSF), is the Department of Defense's (DOD) most costly and ambitious aircraft acquisition, seeking to simultaneously develop and field three aircraft variants for the Air Force, Navy, Marine Corps, and eight international partners. The JSF is critical to DOD's long-term recapitalization plans as it is intended to replace hundreds of legacy fighters and strike aircraft. Total U.S. investment in the JSF will be substantial—approaching $400 billion to develop and acquire 2,457 aircraft over several decades—and will require a long-term sustained funding commitment. Over the last 2 years, the JSF program has been extensively restructured to address relatively poor cost, schedule, and performance outcomes.

We have reported on JSF issues for a number of years.[1] A recurring theme in our body of work since 2005 has been a concern about the substantial concurrency, or overlap, of JSF development, test, and production activities and the heightened risk it poses to achieving good program outcomes. The effects of concurrency became apparent in 2011 as the JSF program incurred an estimated $373 million in additional costs to retrofit already-procured aircraft to correct deficiencies discovered during testing. Our prior reports have also made numerous recommendations for reducing risks and improving chances for successful outcomes; DOD has taken actions on these recommendations to varying degrees. Appendix III summarizes our major prior reports, DOD's responses, and subsequent actions. In April 2011, we reported that the department's restructuring actions should lead to more achievable and predictable outcomes, albeit at higher costs and with extended times to test and deliver capabilities to the warfighter.[2] The report also identified continuing issues concerning affordability risks (both for acquiring JSF aircraft and supporting them over the life-cycle), delays in software development, a continued high rate of design changes, and immature manufacturing processes.

---

[1] See related GAO products at the end of this report .

[2] GAO, *Joint Strike Fighter: Restructuring Places Program on Firmer Footing, but Progress Still Lags*, GAO-11-325 (Washington, D.C.: Apr. 7, 2011).

GAO-12-437 Joint Strike Fighter

The National Defense Authorization Act for Fiscal Year 2010[3] requires GAO to review the JSF program annually for 6 years. In this report, we address (1) program cost and schedule changes and their implications on affordability; (2) performance testing results and technical risks; and (3) contract cost performance, concurrency impacts, and design and manufacturing maturity. This report also includes additional information on the "probation period" and performance of the short takeoff and vertical landing (STOVL) variant as requested by the Senate Armed Services Committee. To conduct this work, we evaluated DOD's restructuring actions and impacts on the program, tracked cost and schedule changes, and determined factors driving the changes. We reviewed program status reports, manufacturing data, test plans, and internal DOD analyses. We discussed results to date and future plans to complete JSF development and move further into procurement with DOD, JSF, and contractor officials. We toured aircraft and engine manufacturing plants, obtained production and supply performance indicators, and discussed improvements underway with contractors and DOD plant representatives. Appendix I contains a more detailed description of our scope and methodology. We conducted this performance audit from June 2011 to June 2012 in accordance with generally accepted government auditing standards. Those standards required that we plan and perform the audit to obtain sufficient, appropriate evidence to provide a reasonable basis for our findings and conclusions based on our audit objectives. We believe that evidence obtained provides a reasonable basis for our findings and conclusions based on our audit objectives.

Background

The JSF is a joint, multinational acquisition to develop and field an affordable, highly common family of next generation strike fighter aircraft for the United States Air Force, Navy, Marine Corps, and eight international partners.[4] The JSF is a single-seat, single engine aircraft incorporating low-observable (stealth) technologies, defensive avionics, advanced sensor fusion,[5] internal and external weapons, and advanced

---

[3] Pub. L. No. 111-84, § 244 (2009).

[4] The international partners are the United Kingdom, Italy, the Netherlands, Turkey, Canada, Australia, Denmark and Norway. These nations are contributing funds for system development and have signed agreements to procure aircraft.

[5] Sensor fusion is the ability to take information from both multiple on-board and off-board aircraft sensors and display the information in an easy-to-use format for the single pilot.

prognostic maintenance capability. There are three variants. The conventional takeoff and landing (CTOL) variant will be an air-to-ground replacement for the Air Force's F-16 Falcon and the A-10 Thunderbolt II aircraft, and will complement the F-22A Raptor. The STOVL variant will be a multi-role strike fighter to replace the Marine Corps' F/A-18C/D Hornet and AV-8B Harrier aircraft. The carrier-suitable variant (CV) will provide the Navy a multi-role, stealthy strike aircraft to complement the F/A-18 E/F Super Hornet.

DOD began the JSF program in October 2001 with a highly concurrent, aggressive acquisition strategy with substantial overlap between development, testing, and production. The program was replanned in 2004 following weight and performance problems and rebaselined in 2007 due to cost growth and schedule slips. In February 2010, the Secretary of Defense announced another comprehensive restructuring of the program due to poor outcomes and continuing problems. This restructuring followed an extensive Department-wide review which included three independent groups chartered to evaluate program execution and resources, manufacturing processes and plans, and engine costs and affordability initiatives. DOD provided additional resources for testing–funding, time, and flight test assets–and reduced near-term procurement by 122 aircraft. As a result of the additional funding needed and recognition of higher unit procurement costs, in March 2010 the Department declared that the program experienced a Nunn-McCurdy breach of the critical cost growth statutory threshold[6] and subsequently certified to the Congress in June 2010 that the JSF program

---

[6] Commonly referred to as Nunn-McCurdy, 10 U.S.C. § 2433 establishes the requirements for DOD to submit unit cost reports on major defense acquisition program or designated major subprograms. Two measures are tracked against the current and original baseline estimates for a program: procurement unit cost (total procurement funds divided by the quantity of systems procured) and program acquisition unit cost (total funds for development, procurement, and system-specific military construction divided by the quantity of systems procured). If a program's procurement unit cost or acquisition unit cost increases by at least 15 percent over the current baseline estimate or at least 30 percent over the original baseline estimate, it constitutes a breach of the significant cost growth threshold. If a program's procurement unit cost or acquisition unit cost increases by at least 25 percent over the current baseline estimate or at least 50 percent over the original baseline estimate, it constitutes a breach of the critical cost growth threshold. Programs are required to notify Congress if a Nunn-McCurdy breach is experienced. When a program experiences a Nunn-McCurdy breach of the critical cost growth threshold, DOD is required to take a number of steps, including reassessing the program and submitting a certification to Congress in order to continue the program, in accordance with 10 U.S.C. § 2433a.

should continue. The program's approval to enter system development was rescinded and efforts commenced to establish a new acquisition program baseline. The new JSF program executive officer subsequently led a comprehensive technical baseline review. In January 2011, the Secretary of Defense announced additional development cost increases, further delays, and cut another 124 aircraft through fiscal year 2016. Restructuring continued throughout 2011 and into 2012, adding to costs and extending the schedules for achieving key activities. The Department's restructuring actions have helped reduce near-term risks by lowering annual procurement quantities and allowing more time and resources for flight testing.

Restructuring Reduces Near Term Risk, but Long Term Affordability is Challenging

In late March 2012, the Department established a new acquisition program baseline and approved the continuation of system development. These decisions, critical for program management and oversight, had been delayed several times and came 2 years after the Department alerted the Congress that the program experienced a breach of the Nunn-McCurdy critical cost growth threshold and thus require a new milestone approval for system development and a new acquisition program baseline. The new JSF baseline projects a total acquisition cost of $395.7 billion, an increase of $117.2 billion (42 percent) from the prior 2007 baseline. Table 1 shows changes in cost, quantity, and schedule since the start of system development (2001), a major redesign (2004), a revised baseline following the program's Nunn-McCurdy breach of the significant cost growth statutory threshold (2007), initial restructuring actions after the Nunn-McCurdy breach of the critical cost growth statutory threshold (2010), and the new acquisition program baseline (2012).

Table 1: JSF Program Cost and Quantity Estimates over Time

	October 2001 (system development start)	December 2003 (2004 replan)	March 2007 (approved baseline)	June 2010 (Nunn-McCurdy)	March 2012 (approved baseline)
Expected quantities					
Development quantities	14	14	15	14	14
Procurement quantities (U.S. only)	2,852	2,443	2,443	2,443	2,443
Total quantities	2,866	2,457	2,458	2,457	2,457
Cost estimates (then-year dollars in billions)					
Development	$34.4	$44.8	$44.8	$51.8	$55.2
Procurement	196.6	199.8	231.7	325.1	335.7
Military construction	2.0	0.2	2.0	5.6	4.8
Total program acquisition	$233.0	$244.8	$278.5	$382.5	$395.7
Unit cost estimates (then-year dollars in millions)					
Program acquisition	$81	$100	$113	$156	$161
Average procurement	69	82	95	133	137
Estimated delivery and production dates					
First production aircraft delivery	2008	2009	2010	2010	2011
Initial operational capability	2010-2012	2012-2013	2012-2015	TBD	TBD
Full-rate production	2012	2013	2013	2016	2019

Source: GAO analysis of DOD data.

Full rate production is now planned for 2019, a delay of 6 years from the 2007 baseline. Unit cost estimates continue to increase and have now doubled since the start of development. Initial operational capability dates for the Air Force, Navy and Marines—the critical dates when the warfighter expects the capability promised by the acquisition program to be available—have slipped over time and are now unsettled.

The fiscal year 2013 defense budget request and five-year plan supports the new approved baseline. Compared to the fiscal year 2012 budget plan for the same time period, the 2013 budget plan identifies $369 million more for JSF development and testing and $14.2 billion less in procurement funding for fiscal years 2012 through 2016. Procurement funding reflects the reduction of 179 aircraft in annual procurement quantities from fiscal year 2013 to fiscal year 2017. Appendix IV summarizes the new budget's development and procurement funding requests and aircraft quantities for each service.

Taken as a whole, the Department's restructuring actions have helped reduce near term acquisition risks by lowering annual procurement quantities and allowing more time and resources for flight testing. However, continuing uncertainties about the program and frequently changing prognoses make it difficult for the United States and international partners to confidently commit to future budgets and procurement schedules, while finalizing related plans for basing JSF aircraft, developing a support infrastructure, and determining force and retirement schedules for legacy aircraft. Over the long haul, affordability is a key challenge. Projected annual acquisition funding needs average more than $12.5 billion through 2037 and life-cycle operating and support costs are estimated at $1.1 trillion.

Development Cost and Schedule Changes

The new baseline increased cost and extended the schedule for completing system development. Development is now expected to cost $55.2 billion, an increase of $10.4 billion (23 percent) from the 2007 baseline. About 80 percent of these funds have been appropriated through fiscal year 2011. System development funding is now required through fiscal year 2018, 5 more years than the 2007 baseline. Figures 1 and 2 track cost increases and major events regarding the aircraft and engine development contracts, respectively.[7]

---

[7] In addition to the aircraft and engine contract costs shown in figures 1 and 2, the total development cost of $55.2 billion in the new baseline includes program management, testing, and other government costs of about $15.0 billion.

Figure 1: JSF Aircraft Development Contract Changes

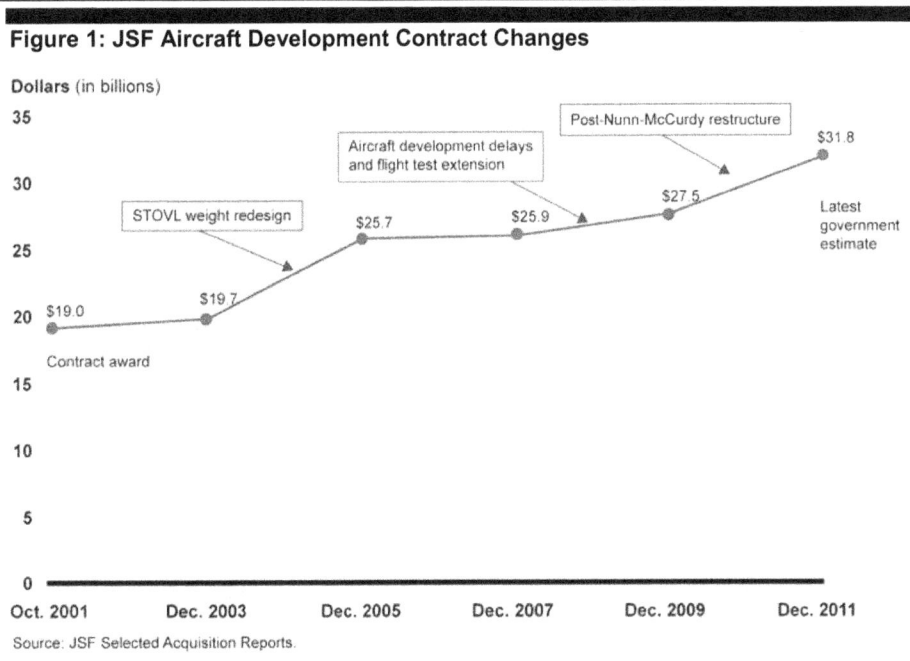

Source: JSF Selected Acquisition Reports.

Figure 2: Primary Engine Development Contract Changes

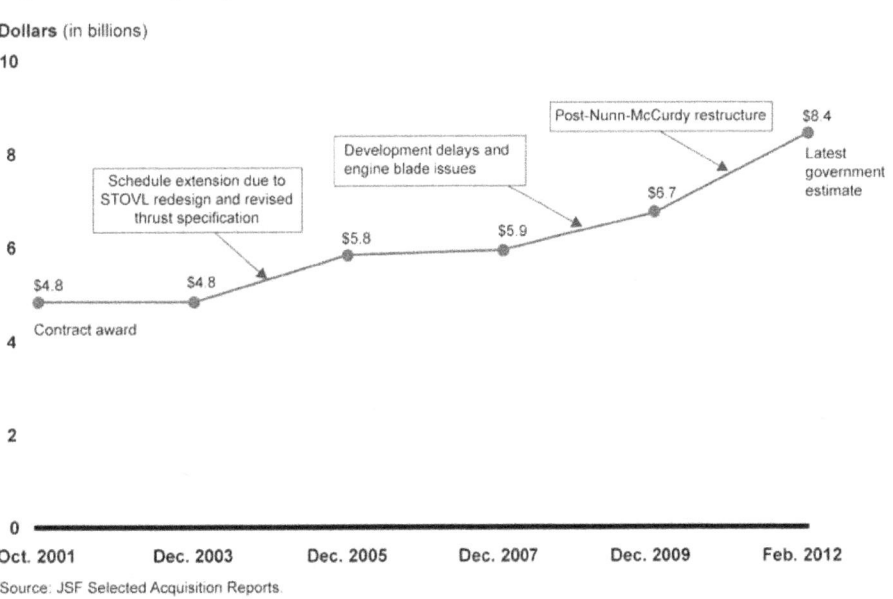

Source: JSF Selected Acquisition Reports.

Procurement Cost and Quantity Changes

The new baseline includes $335.7 billion in procurement funding, an increase of $104 billion (45 percent) compared to the 2007 baseline. About 6 percent of this total funding requirement has been appropriated through fiscal year 2011. Concerned about concurrency risks, DOD, in the fiscal year 2013 budget request, reduced planned procurement quantities through fiscal year 2017 by 179 aircraft. This marked the third time in as many years that near-term procurement quantities had been reduced. Combined with other changes since the 2007 revised baseline, total JSF procurement quantity has been reduced by 410 aircraft through fiscal year 2017. Since the department still plans to eventually acquire the full complement of U.S. aircraft—2,443 production jets—the procurement costs, fielding schedules, and support requirements for the deferred aircraft will be incurred in future years beyond 2017. The new plan also stretches the period of planned procurement another two years to 2037. Figure 3 shows how planned quantities in the near-term have steadily declined over time.

Figure 3: Changes in Procurement Plans over Time

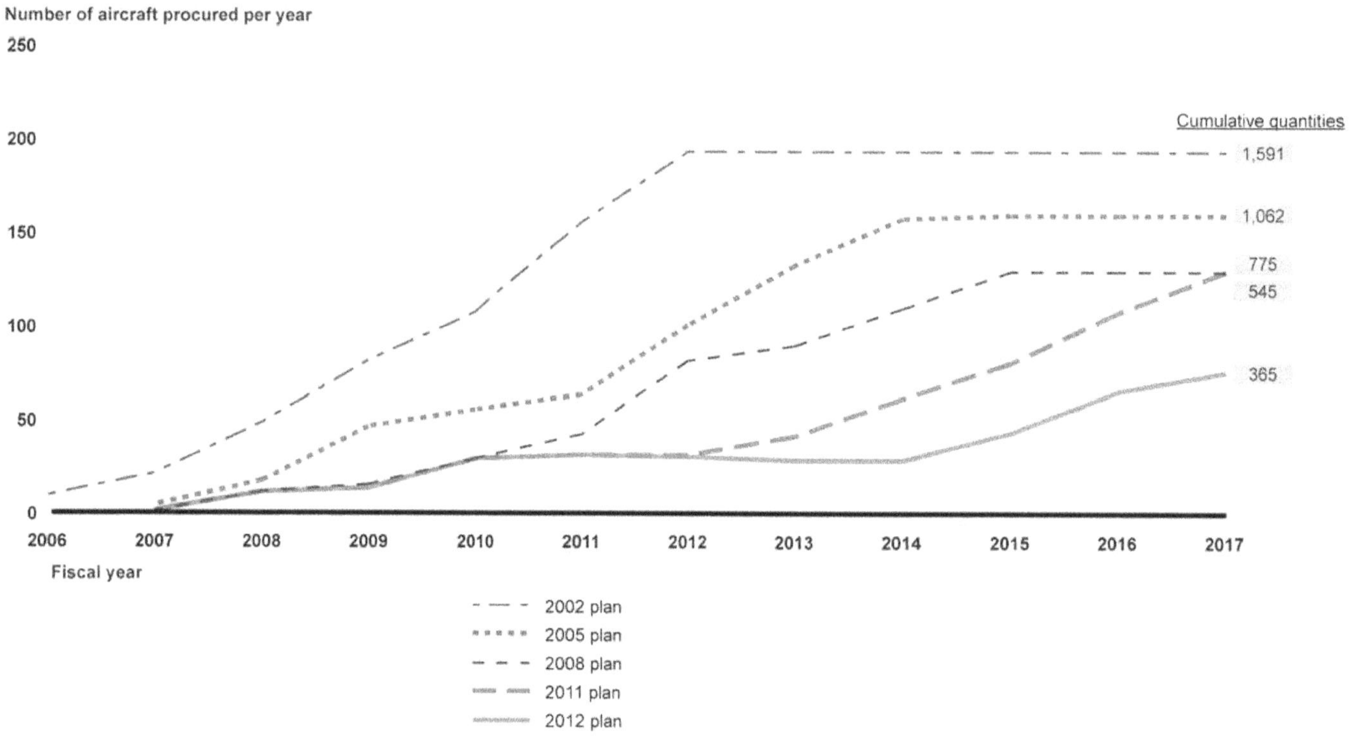
Number of aircraft procured per year
250
200
150
100
50
0
2006
2007
2008
2009
2010
2011
2012
2013
2014
2015
2016
2017
Fiscal year
Cumulative quantities
1,591
1,062
775
545
365
2002 plan
2005 plan
2008 plan
2011 plan
2012 plan

Source: GAO analysis of DOD data.

With the latest reduction, the program now plans to procure a total of 365 aircraft through 2017, about one-fourth of the 1,591 aircraft expected in the 2002 plan. The ramp rate (annual increases in quantities) for the early production years has been significantly flattened over time. Reducing near-term procurement quantities lowers concurrency risks because fewer aircraft are produced that may later need to be modified to correct problems discovered during testing. However, it also means that the number of aircraft and associated capabilities that the program committed to provide the warfighter will be delivered years later than planned.

Affordability Challenges

Overall program affordability—both in terms of the investment costs to acquire the JSF and the continuing costs to operate and maintain it over the life-cycle—remains a major challenge. As shown in figure 4, the annual funding requirements average more than $12.5 billion through 2037 and average more than $15 billion annually in the 10-year period from fiscal years 2019 through 2028. The Air Force alone needs to budget from about $6 to $11 billion per year from fiscal year 2016 through 2037 for procurement of JSF aircraft. At the same time, the Air Force is committed to other big-dollar projects such as the KC-46 tanker and a new bomber program.

Figure 4: JSF Budgeted Development and Procurement Costs

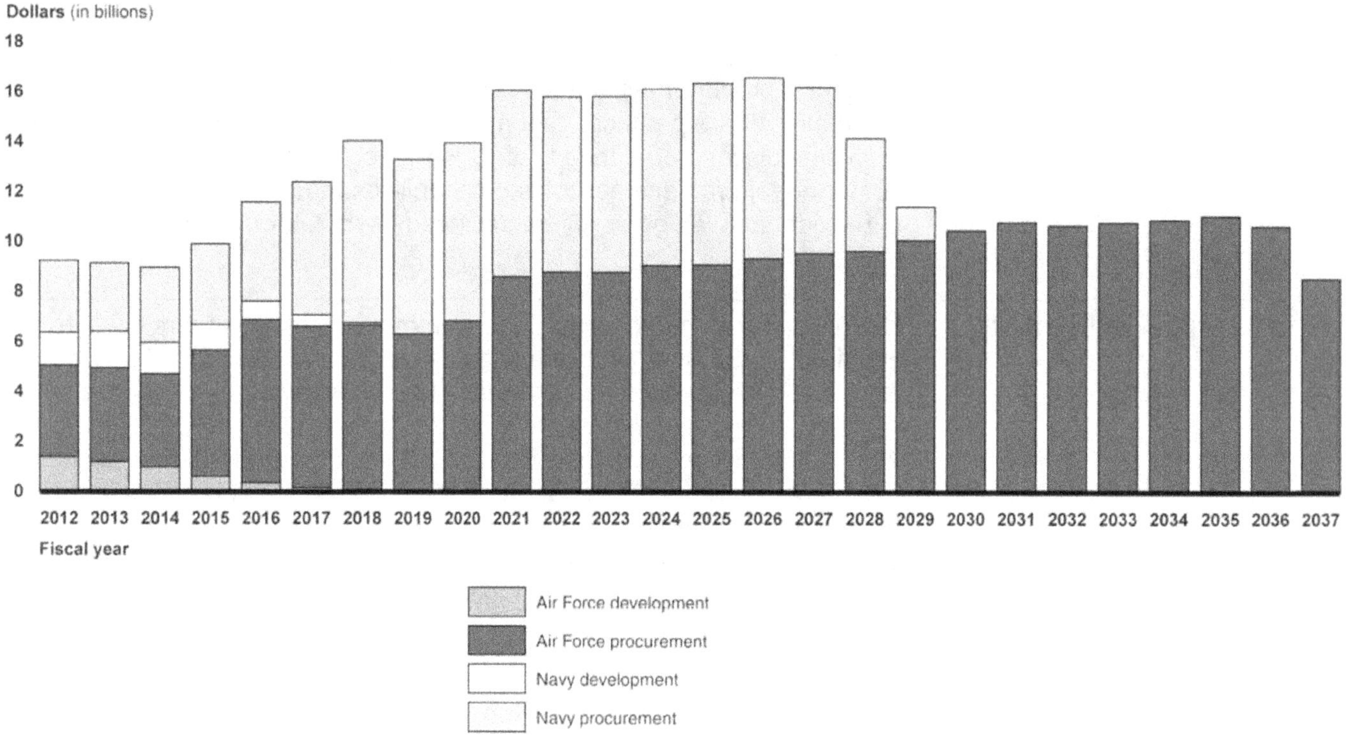

Dollars (in billions)

Fiscal year

Air Force development

Air Force procurement

Navy development

Navy procurement

Source: GAO analysis; JSF Selected Acquisition Report (December 2011).

The long-stated intent that the JSF program would deliver an affordable, highly common fifth generation aircraft that could be acquired in large numbers is at risk. Continued increases in aircraft prices erode buying power and may make it difficult for the U.S. and international partners to buy as many aircraft as planned and to do so within the intended timeframe. As the JSF program moves forward, unprecedented levels of funding will be required during a period of more constrained defense funding expectations overall. If future funding is not available at these projected levels, the impacts on unit costs and program viability are unclear. Program officials have not reported on potential impacts from lowered levels of funding.

In addition to the costs for acquiring aircraft, significant concerns and questions persist regarding the costs to operate and sustain JSF fleets over the coming decades. The most recent estimate projects total United States operating and support costs of $1.1 trillion for all three variants based on a 30-year service life and predicted usage and attrition rates.

Defense leadership stated in 2011 that sustainment cost estimates at this time were unaffordable and simply unacceptable in the current fiscal environment. In March 2012, the Department established affordability targets for sustainment as well as production. The sustainment affordability target for the Air Force's CTOL ($35,200 per flight hour) is much higher than the current cost for the F-16 it will replace ($22,500 per flight hour, both expressed in fiscal year 2012 dollars). Comparative data for the Navy's CV and Marine Corps' STOVL with the legacy aircraft to be replaced was not available. Program officials noted that there are substantive differences between legacy and F-35 operating and funding assumptions which complicate direct cost comparisons. The program has undertaken efforts to address this life-cycle affordability concern. However, until DOD can demonstrate that the program can perform against its cost projections, it will continue to be difficult for the United States and international partners to accurately set priorities, establish affordable procurement rates, retire aged aircraft, and establish supporting infrastructure.

Mixed Performance in 2011 Affected by Concurrency and Technical Risks

Much of the instability in the JSF program has been and continues to be the result of highly concurrent development, testing, and production activities. During 2011, overall performance was mixed as the program achieved 6 of 11 primary objectives for the year. Developmental flight testing gained momentum and had tangible success, but it has a long road ahead with testing of the most complex software and advanced capabilities still in the future. JSF software development is one of the largest and most complex projects in DOD history, providing essential capability, but software has grown in size and complexity, and is taking longer to complete than expected. Developing, testing, and integrating software, mission systems, and logistics systems are critical for demonstrating the operational effectiveness and suitability of a fully integrated, capable aircraft and pose significant technical risks moving forward. Until a fully integrated, capable aircraft is flight tested–planned to start in 2015–the program is still very susceptible to discovering costly design and technical problems after many aircraft have been fielded.

Program Performance Against 2011 Stated Objectives Was Mixed

The JSF program achieved 6 of 11 primary objectives it established for 2011. Five of the objectives were specific test and training actions tied to contractual expectations and award fees, according to program officials. The other 6 objectives were associated with cost, schedule, contract negotiations, and sustainment. The program successfully met 2 important test objectives: the Marine Corps' short takeoff and vertical landing (STOVL) variant accomplished sea trials and the Navy's carrier variant (CV) completed static structural testing. Two other test objectives were not met: software was not released to flight test in time and the carrier variant did not demonstrate shipboard suitability because of problems with the tail hook arrestment system. The program also successfully completed objectives related to sustainment design reviews, schedule data, manufacturing processes, and cost control, but did not meet a training deadline or complete contract negotiations. Table 2 summarizes the 2011 objectives and accomplishments.

Table 2: JSF Program Results for 2011 Objectives

	2011 JSF Program Objectives		
	Objective (Grey shaded objectives are contractual objectives)	**Objective met?**	**Accomplishments**
Test	Complete carrier variant static structural testing	Yes	Executed planned test conditions for CV (CG-1) variant.
	Complete first carrier variant ship suitability events	No	Suitability testing was not completed; tail hook did not successfully engage the cable during ground testing.
	Release initial Block 2A software to flight test	No	Did not complete timely Block 2 software release. Block 2A is flying on surrogate aircraft, with initial Block 2A F-35 flights in January 2012 pending a successful Air System Test Readiness Review.
	Execute short take-off and landing variant sea trials on amphibious assault ship	Yes	Executed F-35B sea trials focused on flying qualities and performance tests, vertical landing to designated locations, and external environment effects on the ship.
Training/ sustainment	Deliver Block 1 training update to Eglin (capability, envelope, trainers, autonomic logistics information system)	No	Did not complete Block 1 training update to Eglin Air Force Base. Operations to practice and validate training profiles, maintenance procedures, and build maturity are expected to begin in early 2012, with a software Block 1A operational utility evaluation and declaration of training readiness to follow. Block 1B training will follow Block 1A readiness.
	Complete sustainment design reviews, cost and strategy bottoms up	Yes	Completed design review of the supply chain management concept for F-35, third war game effort, and business case analysis phase 1 for sustainment strategy; further developed sustainment baseline; and completed a review of ground rules and assumptions to support a revised operations and support cost estimate.
Contract	Complete over target baseline negotiations	No	Program did not gain agreement on new prime and engine contractor program management baselines to complete system development and demonstration or negotiate contract modifications to update cost and schedule positions. The program is finalizing details to begin negotiations in early 2012.
	Negotiate Low Rate Initial Production (LRIP) 5 production contract	No	Program did not complete negotiations and sign a definitized LRIP 5 production contract. The program executed an undefinitized[a] LRIP 5 contract action, which included completed negotiations on contract terms and conditions concerning concurrency cost sharing.
Cost/Schedule	Observe LRIP 4 cost control	Yes[b]	Program observed cost control with LRIP 4 production activities. Projected average percent overrun for LRIP 4 aircraft is lower than the previous LRIP buys.
	Populate prime contractor EVMS data with new re-planned schedule	Yes	Program office and prime contractor agreed on a new prime contractor system development and demonstration program performance measurement baseline, loaded the cost/schedule position, and began reporting against the baseline.
	Observe prime contractor delivering assembled wings and forward fuselage to mate station on time at reduced cost	Yes	Prime contractor agreed to delivery dates for LRIP 4 wing and forward fuselage; kept LRIP 4 average aircraft cost lower than LRIPs 2/3; reduced number of quality assurance reports, improved quality, and minimized rework; reduced span times without increasing of out-of-station work; and achieved contract target cost.

Source: JSF Program Office Data.

[a] An undefinitized contract action means any contract action for which the contract terms, specifications, or price are not agreed upon before performance is begun under the action. Defense Federal Acquisition Regulation Supplement section 217.7401(d).

[b] Program officials consider this objective met for the reason stated above. We note that the current size of the overrun is considerable and that it could very well change for better or worse as this lot is still early in the production process.

Development Flight Testing Gained Momentum

Development flight testing gained momentum and met or exceeded most objectives in its modified test plan for 2011. The program accomplished 972 test flights in 2011, more than double the flights in 2010. Final deliveries of the remaining test aircraft were made in 2011 (with the exception of one carrier variant added in restructuring and expected in 2012) and five production aircraft have been made available to the test program. Flight test points[8] accomplished in 2011 exceeded the plan overall, as shown in figure 5. CTOL flight test points achieved fell short of the plan, due to operating limitations and aircraft reliability.

Figure 5: 2011 JSF Flight Test Points Progress

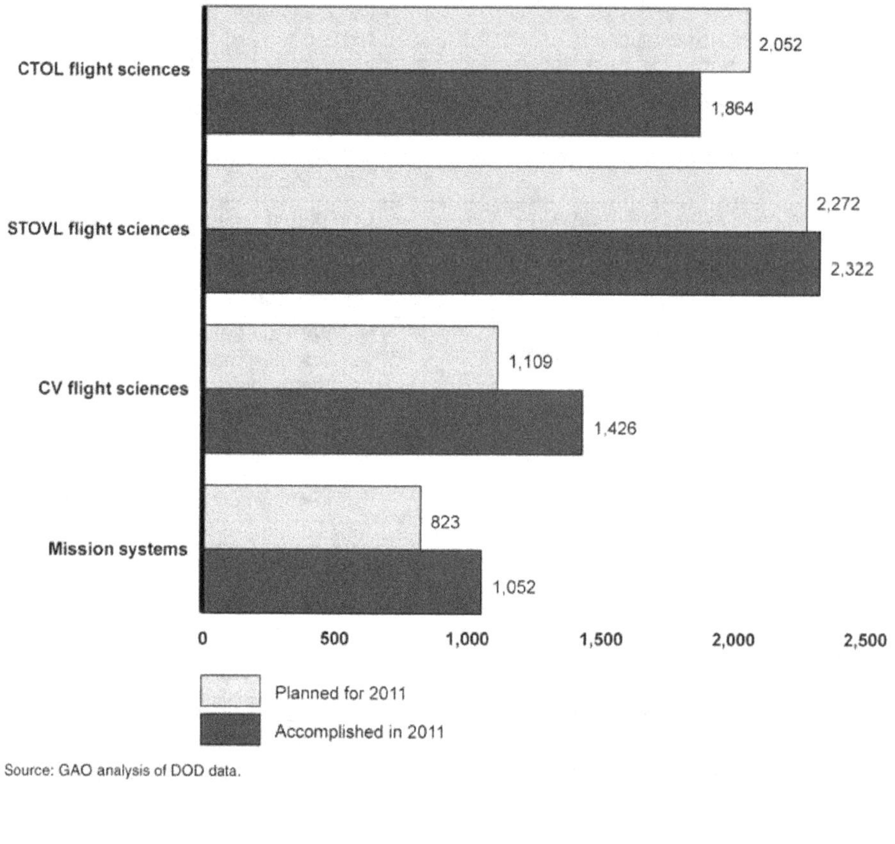

Source: GAO analysis of DOD data.

[8] Flight test points are specific, quantifiable objectives in flight plans that are needed to verify aircraft design and performance.

Flight testing during 2011 included the following results:

- Navy's Carrier Variant: The program successfully accomplished 65 catapult launches, but problems with the arresting hook prevented successful engagement with the cable during ground testing. Analysis of test results discovered tail hook design issues that have major consequences, according to DOD officials. The tail hook point is being redesigned and other aircraft structural modifications may also be required. The program must have fixes in place and deficiencies resolved in order to accomplish CV ship trials in late 2013. Since the carrier variant has just started initial carrier suitability tests, the proposed design changes will not be demonstrated until much later in developmental testing and could require significant structural changes to already-delivered aircraft. According to officials from the office of the Director, Operational Test and Evaluation (DOT&E), the program is also working to correct a number of other carrier variant performance problems such as excessive nose gear oscillations during taxi operations, excessive landing gear retraction times, and overheating of the electro-hydrostatic actuator systems that power flight controls. The program has not yet determined if production aircraft will need to be modified to address these issues.

- Air Force's Conventional Takeoff and Landing Variant: The JSF test team flew the planned number of CTOL flights in 2011 but achieved about 10 percent fewer flight sciences test points than planned. Aircraft operating limitations and inadequate instrumentation impacted the ability to complete the planned number of test points. Contributing factors included deficiencies in the air vehicle's air data system as well as in-flight data indicating different structural loads than predicted. Aircraft reliability and parts shortages also affected the number of CTOL flight tests.

- Marine Corps's Short Take Off and Vertical Landing Variant: The STOVL variant performed better than expected in flight tests during 2011. It increased flight test rates and STOVL-specific mode testing, surpassing planned test point progress for the year. Following reliability problems and performance issues, the Secretary of Defense in January 2011 had placed the STOVL on "probation" for up to two years, citing technical issues unique to the variant that would add to the aircraft's cost and weight. In January 2012, the Secretary of Defense lifted the STOVL probation after one year, citing improved performance and completion of the initial sea trials as a basis for the decision. The Department concluded that STOVL development, test, and production maturity is now comparable to the other two variants.

While several technical issues have been addressed and some potential solutions engineered, assessing whether the deficiencies are resolved is ongoing and, in some cases, will not be known for years. According to the program office, two of the five specific problems cited are considered to be fixed while the other three have temporary fixes in place. (See Appendix V which provides a more detailed examination of the STOVL probation, deficiencies addressed, and plans for correcting deficiencies.) DOT&E officials reported that significant work remains to verify and incorporate modifications to correct known STOVL deficiencies and prepare the system for operational use. Until the proposed technical solutions have been fully tested and demonstrated, it cannot be determined if the technical problems have been resolved.

Even with the progress in 2011, most development flight testing, including the most challenging, still lies ahead. Through 2011, the flight test program had completed 21 percent of the nearly 60,000 planned flight test points estimated for the entire program.[9] Program officials reported that flight tests to date have largely demonstrated air worthiness, flying qualities, and initial speed, altitude, and maneuvering performance requirements. According to JSF test officials, the more complex testing such as low altitude flight operations, weapons and mission systems integration, and high angle of attack has yet to be done for any variant and may result in new discoveries of aircraft deficiencies. Initial development flight tests of a fully integrated, capable JSF aircraft to demonstrate full mission systems capabilities, weapons delivery, and autonomic logistics is not expected until 2015 at the earliest. This will be critical for verifying that the JSF aircraft will work as intended and for demonstrating that the design is not likely to need costly changes. Development flight testing in a production-representative test aircraft and in the operational flight environment planned for the JSF is important to reducing risk. This actual environment differs from what can be demonstrated in the laboratory and has historically identified unexpected problems. For example, the F-22A fighter software worked as expected in the laboratory, but significant problems were identified in flight tests. These problems delayed testing and the delivery of a proven capability to the warfighter. Like other major weapon systems acquisitions, the JSF will

---

[9] According to program officials, completion of a test point means that the test point has been flown and that flight engineers ruled that the point has met the need. Further analysis may be necessary for the test point to be closed out.

be susceptible to discovering costly problems later in development when the more complex software and advanced capabilities are integrated and flight tested. With most development flight testing still to go, the program can expect more changes to aircraft design and continued alterations of manufacturing processes.

Initial dedicated operational testing of a fully integrated and capable JSF is scheduled to begin in 2017. Initial operational testing is important for evaluating the effectiveness and suitability of the JSF in an operationally realistic environment. It is a prerequisite for JSF full-rate production decision in 2019. The JSF operational test team[10] assessed system readiness for initial operational testing and identified several outstanding risk items. The test team's operational assessment concluded that the JSF is not on track to meet operational effectiveness or operational suitability requirements. The test team's October 2011 report identified deficiencies in the helmet mounted display, night vision capability, aircraft handling characteristics, and shortfalls in maneuvering performance. Test officials also reported an inadequate logistics system for deployments, excessive time for low observable repair and restoration, low reliability, and poor maintainability performance. The team's report noted that many of the concerns that drive the program's readiness for operational test and evaluation are also critical path items to meet effectiveness and suitability requirements.

In its 2011 annual report, DOT&E reported many challenges for the JSF program due to the high level of concurrency of production, development, and test activities. Flight training efforts were delayed because of immature aircraft. Durability testing identified structural modifications needed for production aircraft to meet service life and operational requirements. Analysis of the bulkhead crack problem revealed numerous other life-limited parts on all three variants. According to DOT&E's report, the most significant of these deficiencies in terms of complexity, aircraft downtime, and difficulty in modification required for existing aircraft is the forward wing root rib which experienced cracking during CTOL durability testing. STOVL variant aircraft are also affected. Production aircraft in the first four lots (63 aircraft) will need the modification before these aircraft reach their forward root rib operating limits, which program officials

---

[10] The JSF Operational Test Team consists of members from the Air Force Test and Evaluation Center, the Navy's Operational Test and Evaluation Force, and the United Kingdom's Air Warfare Centre.

identified as 574 flight hours for the CTOL and 750 hours for the STOVL. DOT&E also found that, although it is early in the program, current reliability and maintainability data indicate that more attention is needed in these areas to achieve an operationally suitable system. Its report also highlighted several discoveries which included deficiencies in the helmet mounted display, STOVL door and propulsion problems, limited progress in demonstrating mission systems capabilities, and challenges in managing weight growth.

Software Development and Integration Represent Significant Risks

Software providing essential JSF capability has grown in size and complexity, and is taking longer to complete than expected. Late releases of software have delayed testing and training and added costs. Some capabilities have been deferred until later in development in order to maintain schedule.

The lines of code necessary for the JSF's capabilities have now grown to over 24 million—9.5 million on-board the aircraft. (By comparison, JSF has about 3 times more on-board software lines of code than the F-22A Raptor and 6 times more than the F/A-18 E/F Super Hornet.) This has added work and increased the overall complexity of the effort. The software on-board the aircraft and needed for operations has grown 37 percent since the critical design review in 2005. While software growth appears to be stabilizing, contractor officials report that almost half of the on-board software has yet to complete integration and test—typically the most challenging phase of software development. JSF software growth is not much different than other recent defense acquisitions, which have experienced from 30 to 100 percent growth in software code over time. However, the sheer number of lines of code for the JSF makes the growth a notable cost and schedule challenge. Figure 6 shows increased lines of code for both airborne and ground systems.

Figure 6: Software Growth

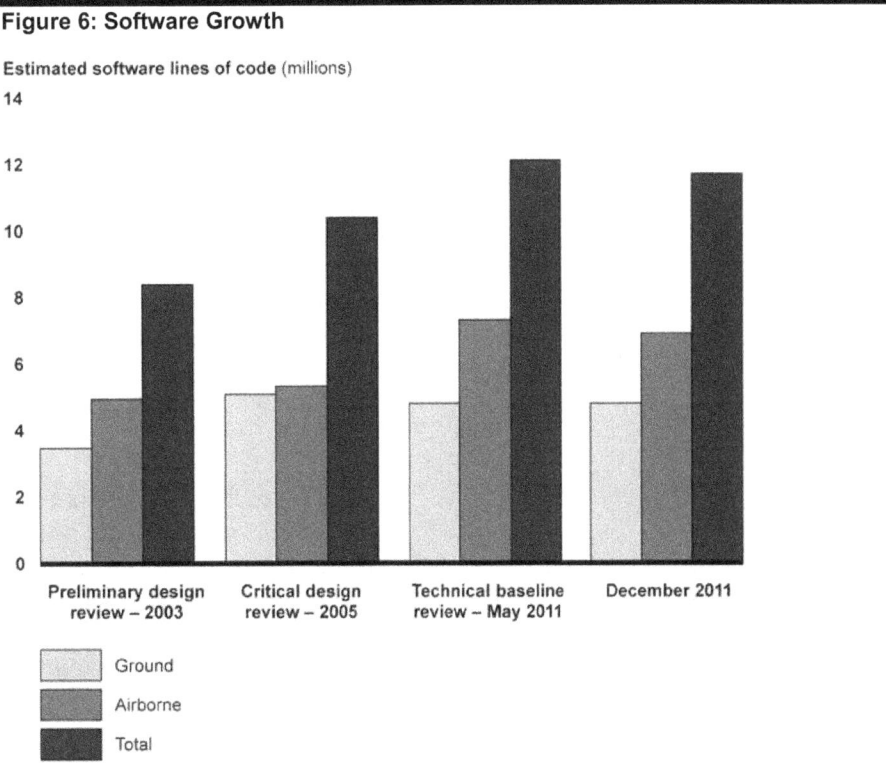

Estimated software lines of code (millions)

Source: GAO analysis of DOD data.

JSF software capabilities are developed, integrated, tested, and delivered to aircraft in 5 increments or blocks. Software defects, low productivity, and concurrent development of successive blocks have created inefficiencies, taking longer to fix defects and delaying the demonstration of critical capabilities. Delays in developing, integrating, and releasing software to the test program have cascading effects hampering flight tests, training, and test lab accreditation. While progress has been made, a substantial amount of software work remains before the program can demonstrate full warfighting capability. Block 0.1, providing flight science capabilities for test aircraft, was released about six months late and block 0.5, providing basic flight systems, was almost two years late, due largely to integration problems. Status of the other 3 blocks follows:

- Block 1.0 provides initial training capability and was released to flight test three years late when compared to the 2006 plan. More recently, it began flight test three months late based on the new plan, and was delayed by defects, workload bottlenecks, and security approvals. Late delivery of block 1.0 to training resulted in the program missing one of its key goals for 2011. Block 1.0 was planned to complete testing and be delivered to training in 2011. Full block 1.0 flight testing was only 25 percent complete at that time and fewer than half of the final block 1.0 capabilities (12 of 35) had met full contract verification requirements for aircraft delivery, according to officials.

- Block 2.0 provides initial warfighting capability, including weapons employment, electronic attack, and interoperability. Its full release to testing is now expected in late 2013, over three years later than planned in 2006. Development has fallen behind due to integration challenges and the reallocation of resources to fix block 1.0. As of December 2011, block 2.0 has completed only half of the planned schedule, leaving approximately 70 percent of integration work to complete.

- Block 3.0 provides the full capability required by the warfighter, including full sensor fusion and additional weapons. In its early stage, development and integration is slightly behind schedule with 30 percent of initial block 3.0 having completed the development phase. These challenges will continue as the program develops, integrates, and tests the increasingly complex mission systems software work that lies ahead.

To maintain schedule, the program has deferred some capabilities to later blocks. For example, initial air to ground capabilities were deferred from block 1.0 to 2.0, and several data fusion elements moved from block 2.0 to 3.0. Deferring tasks to later phases of the development program adds more pressure and costs to future software management efforts. It also likely increases the probability of defects being realized later in the program when the more complex capabilities in these later blocks are already expected to be a substantial technical challenge. Recently, some weapons were moved earlier in the plan, from block 3.0 to 2.0, to provide more combat capability in earlier production aircraft.

Because software is critical to the delivery of war fighter capabilities and presents complex cost, schedule and performance challenges, we recommended in our April 2011 report that an independent review of software development, integration, and testing–similar to the review of manufacturing processes–be undertaken. An initial contractor study was recently completed that focused on mission systems' staffing, development, defects, and rework. Program officials are currently implementing several improvement initiatives and plan to broaden the assessment to off-board software development efforts including logistics and training.

Mission Systems and Logistics Systems Maturity Will Be Key for Demonstrating JSF Operational Effectiveness and Suitability

JSF's mission systems[11] and logistics systems are critical to realizing the operational and support capabilities expected by the warfighter, but the hardware and software for these systems are immature and unproven at this time. For example, only 4 percent of mission systems requirements planned in system development and demonstration have been verified. Significant learning and development remains before the program can demonstrate mature mission systems software and hardware, not expected until block 3.0 is delivered in 2015. The program has experienced significant challenges developing and integrating mission systems software. Mission systems hardware has also experienced several technical challenges, including problems with the radar, integrated processor, communication and navigation equipment, and electronic warfare capabilities.

The helmet mounted display in particular continues to have significant technical deficiencies that make it less functional than legacy equipment. The display is integral to the mission systems architecture, reducing pilot workload, and the overall JSF concept of operations—displaying key aircraft performance information as well as tactical situational awareness and weapons employment information on the pilot's helmet visor, replacing conventional heads-up display systems. Helmet problems include integration of the night vision capability, display jitter, and latency (or delay) in transmitting sensor data.[12] These shortfalls may lead to a helmet unable to fully meet warfighter requirements—unsuitable for flight tasks and weapon delivery, as well as creating an unmanageable pilot workload, and may place limitations on the JSF's operational environment, according to program officials. The program office is pursuing a dual path to compensate for the technical issues by developing a second, less capable helmet while trying to fix the first helmet design; this development effort will cost more than $80 million. The selected helmet will not be integrated into the baseline aircraft until

---

[11] Mission systems provide combat effectiveness through next generation sensors with fused information from on-board and off-board systems (i.e. Electronic Warfare, Communication Navigation Identification, Electro-Optical Target System, Electro-Optical Distributed Aperture System, Radar, and Data Links).

[12] Latency is a perceivable discrepancy or lag that occurs between a physical input (e.g. head movement) and the time it takes the computer to recalibrate with a corresponding change. This is the result of system delay including the head tracker delay, computer graphic delay, and display delay. Display jitter is the undesired shaking of display, making symbology unreadable under those conditions. Regarding the JSF, jitter results from worse than expected vibrations, known as aircraft buffet.

2014 or later, increasing the risks of a major system redesign, retrofits of already built aircraft, or changes in concepts of operation.

The Autonomic Logistics Information System (ALIS) is an integral part of the JSF system and serves as an information portal to JSF-unique and external systems, implements and automates logistics processes, and provides decision aids to reduce support resources such as manpower and spares. The ALIS is key technology aimed at improving and streamlining logistics and maintenance functions in order to reduce life cycle costs. It is designed to be proactive–recognize problems and initiate correct responses automatically. The JSF test team operational assessment report concluded that an early release model of ALIS was not mature, did not meet operational suitability requirements, and would require substantial improvements to achieve sortie generation rates and life cycle cost requirements. In particular, the current configuration was not adequate for deployed operations–its current weight, environmental support, connectivity, and security requirements make it difficult to support detachments, operational testing, and forward operations, especially vital to the Marine Corps plans. The report noted that there is no approved concept or design for this capability, no funding identified, and stated a concern that there may be no formal solution prior to Marine Corps declaring an initial operating capability. Operational testers also identified concerns about data and interoperability with service maintenance systems. Program officials have identified deployable ALIS as a development-funded effort structured to address the difficulties surrounding the deployment of the current ALIS suite of equipment. The formal solution is expected to be ready for fielding in 2015.

Contract Overruns and Concurrency Costs Indicate the Program Has Not Yet Stabilized Design and Manufacturing

The program has not yet demonstrated a stable design and manufacturing process capable of efficient production. Engineering changes are persisting at relatively high rates and additional changes will be needed as testing continues. Manufacturing processes and performance indicators show some progress, but performance on the first four low-rate initial production contracts has not been good. All four have experienced cost overruns and late aircraft deliveries. In addition, the government is also incurring substantial additional costs to retrofit produced aircraft to correct deficiencies discovered in testing. Until manufacturing processes are in control and engineering design changes resulting from information gained during developmental testing are reduced, there is risk of further cost growth. Actions the Department has taken to restructure the program have helped, but remaining concurrency between flight testing and production continues to put cost and schedule at risk (see figure 7). Even with the substantial reductions in near-term procurement quantities, DOD is still investing billions of dollars on hundreds of aircraft while flight testing has years to go.

Figure 7: JSF Concurrency

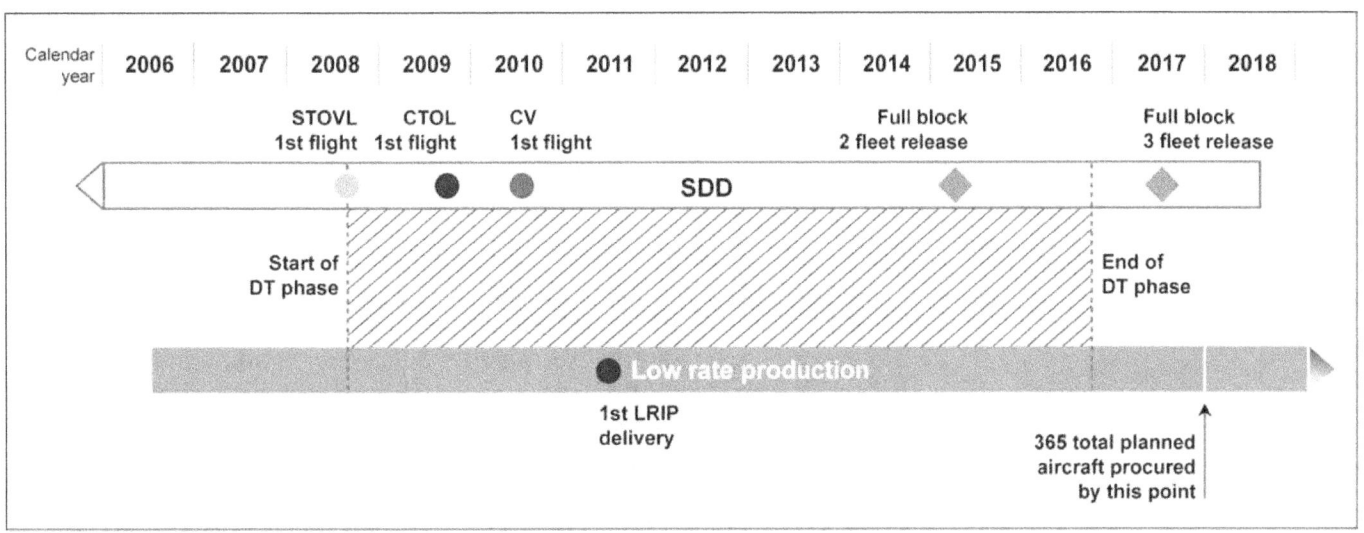

Source: GAO analysis of DOD data.

Note: SDD= system development and demonstration; DT = developmental test.

Cost Overruns and Delivery Delays Indicate Need to Further Mature the Manufacturing Process

As was the experience with building the development test aircraft, manufacturing the production aircraft is costing more and taking longer than planned. Cost overruns and delivery slips indicate that manufacturing processes, worker learning, quality control, and supplier performance are not yet sufficiently mature to handle the volume of work scheduled. Cost overruns on each of the first four annual procurement contracts are currently projected to total about $1 billion (see table 3).

Table 3: Procurement Contract Costs as of January 2012

Dollars in millions

Contract	Number of aircraft	Contract cost at award	Current contract cost estimate	Cost increase	Percent increase
LRIP 1	2	$511.7	$561.5	$49.8	9.7
LRIP 2	12	$2,278.5	$2,607.7	$329.2	14.4
LRIP 3	17	$3,154.2	$3,569.5	$415.3	13.2
LRIP 4	32	$3,458.3	$3,703.3	$245.0	7.1
Total	**63**	**$9,402.7**	**$10,442.0**	**$1,039.3**	**11.1**

Source: GAO analysis of DOD data.

Note: LRIP is low rate initial production.

According to program documentation, through the cost sharing provisions in these contracts, the government's share of the total overrun is about $672 million. On average, the government is paying an additional $11 million for each of the 63 aircraft under contract (58 are U.S. aircraft and 5 are for international partners). There is risk of additional cost overruns because all work is not completed. Defense officials reduced the buy quantity in the fifth annual procurement contract to help fund these cost overruns and additional retrofit costs to fix deficiencies discovered in testing.

While Lockheed Martin, the prime contractor, is demonstrating somewhat better throughput capacity and showing improved performance indicators, the lingering effects of critical parts shortages, out of station work[13], and quality issues continue to be key cost and schedule drivers on the first four production lots. Design modifications to address deficiencies discovered in testing, incorporation of bulkhead and wing process improvements, and reintroduction of the carrier variant into the manufacturing line further impacted production during 2011. Lockheed had expected to deliver 31 procurement aircraft by the end of 2011 but delivered only nine aircraft. Each was delivered more than 1 year late.

The manufacturing effort has a long way to go with thousands of aircraft planned for production over the next 25 years. Through fiscal year 2011,

---

[13] Out of station work occurs when manufacturing steps are not completed at the designated work station and must be finished elsewhere later in production. This is highly inefficient, increasing labor hours, causing delays, and sometimes quality problems.

only 6 percent of the total procurement funding needed to complete the JSF program had been appropriated. As the rate of production is expected to increase substantially starting in 2015, it is vital that the contractor achieve an efficient manufacturing process. Several positive accomplishments may spur improved future performance. Lockheed implemented an improved and comprehensive integrated master schedule, loaded the new program data from restructuring, and completed a schedule risk assessment, as we recommended several years ago.[14] Also, Defense Contract Management Agency (DCMA) and JSF program officials believe that Lockheed Martin has made a concerted effort to improve its earned value management system (EVMS)[15] in order to comply with federal standards. Initial reviews of the new procedures, tools, and training indicate that the company is on track to have its revised processes approved by DCMA this year.

Pratt & Whitney, the engine manufacturer, has delivered 54 production engines and 21 lift fans as of early May 2012.[16] Like the aircraft system, the propulsion system is still under development and the program is working to complete testing and fix deficiencies while concurrently delivering engines under the initial procurement contracts. The program office's estimated cost for the system development and demonstration of the engine has increased by 73 percent, from $4.8 billion to about $8.4 billion, since the start of development. Engine deliveries continue to miss expected contract due dates but still met aircraft need dates. Supplier performance problems and design changes are driving late engine deliveries. Lift fan system components and processes are driving cost and schedule problems.

Going forward, effectively managing the expanding global supplier network – which consists of hundreds of suppliers around the world–is

---

[14] GAO-08-388 and GAO-09-303.

[15] The Earned Value Management System is an important tool that can provide objective production data, track actual costs to budgets, and project contract costs at completion. DOD requires its use by major defense suppliers to facilitate good insight and oversight of the expenditure of government dollars, thereby improving both affordability and accountability. In 2007, DCMA found that Lockheed was deficient in meeting 19 of 32 required guidelines, calling into question its ability to manage the escalating costs and complex scheduling of the JSF program.

[16] Note: The engine contractor has production contracts with the government and the engines are provided as government furnished equipment to the JSF prime contractor.

fundamental to meeting production rate and throughput expectations. DOD's Independent Manufacturing Review Team 2009 report identified global supply chain management as the most critical challenge for meeting production expectations. The cooperative aspect of the supply chain provides both benefits and challenges. The international program structure is based on a complex set of relationships involving both government and industry from the United States and eight other countries. Overseas suppliers are playing a major and increasing role in JSF manufacturing and logistics. For example, center fuselage and wings will be manufactured by Turkish and Italian suppliers, respectively, as second sources. In addition to ongoing supplier challenges–parts shortages, failed parts, and late deliveries– incorporating international suppliers presents other challenges. The program must deal with exchange rate fluctuations, disagreements over work shares, and technology transfer concerns. To date, the mostly U.S.-based suppliers have sometimes struggled to develop critical and complex parts while others have had problems with limited production capacity. Lockheed Martin has implemented a stricter supplier assessment program to help manage supplier performance.

Testing and Production Overlap Increases Engineering Changes and Concurrency Costs

We and some defense offices cautioned the Department years ago about the risks posed by the extremely high degree of concurrency, or overlap, among the JSF development, testing, and production activities.[17] In the first four production lots, the U. S. government will incur an estimated $373 million in retrofit costs on already-built aircraft to correct deficiencies discovered in development testing. This is in addition to the $672 million for the government's share of contract cost overruns. The program office projects additional retrofit costs due to concurrency through the 10th low rate initial production contract, but at decreasing amounts. Questions about who will pay for additional retrofit costs under the fixed price contract–the contractor or the government–and how much, delayed contract negotiations on the fifth lot. While the contract is not yet definitized, a December 2011 undefinitized contract action established that the Government and contractor would share equally in known concurrency costs and that any newly discovered concurrency changes

---

[17] GAO, *Joint Strike Fighter: DOD Plans to Enter Production before Testing Demonstrates Acceptable Performance*, GAO-06-356 (Washington, D.C.: Mar. 15, 2006) and GAO, *Joint Strike Fighter: Progress Made and Challenges Remain*, GAO-07-360 (Washington, D.C.: Apr. 2, 2007).

will be added to the contract and will cause a renegotiation of the target cost, but with no profit, according to program officials.

Defense officials have long acknowledged the substantial concurrency built into the JSF acquisition strategy, but until recently stated that risks were manageable. However, a recent high-level departmental review of JSF concurrency determined that the program is continuing to find problems at a rate more typical of early design experience on previous aircraft development programs, questioning the assumed design maturity that supported the highly concurrent acquisition strategy.[18] DOD's November 2011 report concluded that the "team assesses the current confidence in the design maturity of the F-35 to be lower than one would expect given the quantity of LRIP aircraft procurements planned and the potential cost of reworking these aircraft as new test discoveries are made. This lack of confidence, in conjunction with the concurrency driven consequences of the required fixes, supports serious reconsideration of procurement and production planning." The review identified substantial risk of needed modifications to already produced aircraft as the flight testing enters into more strenuous test activities.

Already, as a result of problems found in less strenuous basic airworthiness testing, critical design modifications are being fed back through the production line. For example, the program will be cutting in aircraft modifications to address bulkhead cracks discovered during airframe ground testing and STOVL auxiliary inlet door durability issues. More critical test discoveries are likely as the program moves into the more demanding phases of testing. We note also that concurrency risks are not just limited to incurring extra production costs, but ripple throughout the JSF program slowing aircraft deliveries, decreasing availability of aircraft, delaying pilot and maintainer training, and hindering the stand-up of base maintenance and supply activities, among other impacts.

Producing aircraft before testing sufficiently demonstrates the design is mature increases the likelihood that more aircraft will be exposed to the need for the retrofit of future design changes, which drives cost growth, schedule delays, and manufacturing inefficiencies. Design changes

---

[18] *F-35 Joint Strike Fighter Concurrency Quick Look Review*, Office of the Undersecretary of Defense for Acquisition, Technology and Logistics, November 29, 2011.

needed in one JSF variant could also impact the other two variants, reducing efficiencies necessary to lower production and operational costs with common parts and manufacturing processes for the three variants. While the JSF program's engineering change traffic–the monthly volume of changes made to engineering drawings–is declining, it is still higher than expected for a program entering its sixth year of production. The total number of engineering drawings continues to grow due to design changes, discoveries during ground and flight testing, and other revisions to drawings. Some level of design change is expected during the production cycle of any new and highly technical product, but excessive changes raise questions about the stability of the JSF's design and its readiness for higher levels of production. Figure 8 tracks design changes over time and shows that changes are expected to persist at an elevated pace through 2019.

Figure 8: JSF Design Changes Over Time

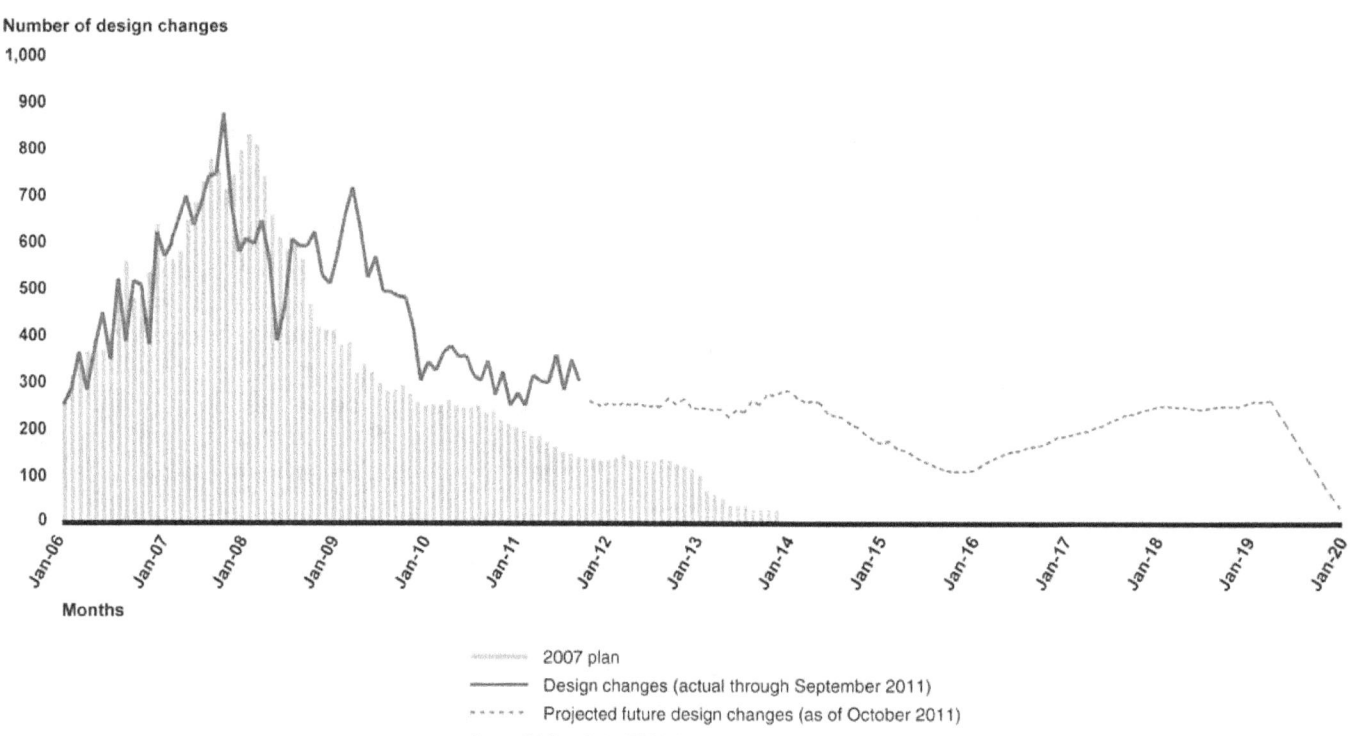

Number of design changes

2007 plan
Design changes (actual through September 2011)
Projected future design changes (as of October 2011)

Source: GAO analysis of DOD data

A weapon system's reliability growth rate is a good indicator of design maturity. Reliability is a function of specific design characteristics. A weapon system is considered reliable when it can perform over a specified period of time without failure, degradation, or need of repair. During system acquisition, reliability growth improvements should occur over time through a process of testing, analyzing, and fixing deficiencies through design changes or manufacturing process improvements. Once fielded, there are limited opportunities to improve a system's reliability without costly redesign and retrofit. A system's reliability rate directly affects its life cycle operating and support costs. We have reported in the past that it is important to demonstrate that the system reliability is on track to meet goals before production begins as changes after production commences can be inefficient and costly.[19]

According to program office data, the CTOL and STOVL variants are behind expected reliability growth plans at this point in the program. Figure 9 depicts progress of each variant in demonstrating mean flying hours between failures as reported by the program office in October 2011 and compares them to 2010 rates, the expectation at this point in time, and the ultimate goal at maturity.

[19] GAO, *Best Practices: Capturing Design and Manufacturing Knowledge Early Improves Acquisition Outcomes*, GAO-02-701 (Washington, D.C.: July 15, 2002).

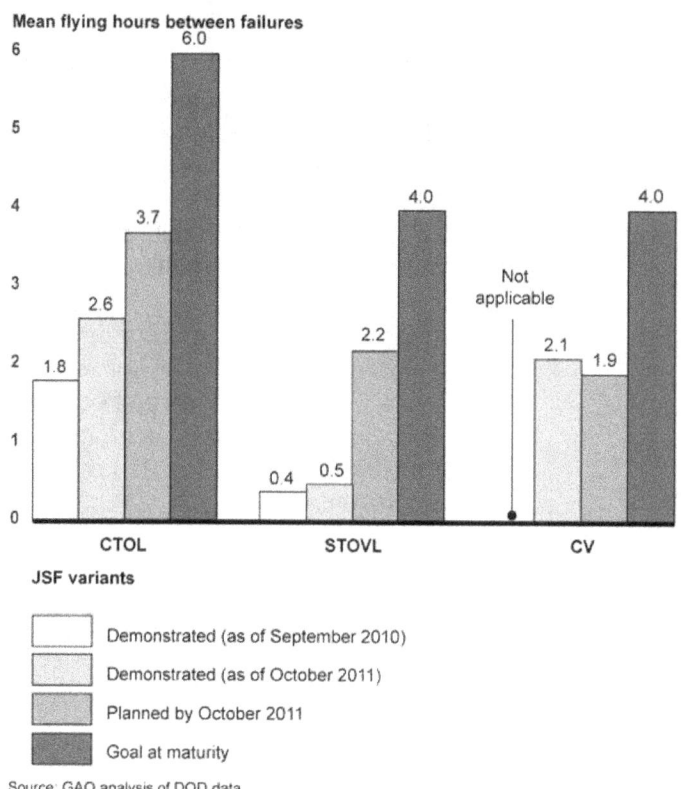

Figure 9: JSF Mean Times between Failure Demonstrated to Date

Mean flying hours between failures

JSF variants

☐ Demonstrated (as of September 2010)
☐ Demonstrated (as of October 2011)
☐ Planned by October 2011
■ Goal at maturity

Source: GAO analysis of DOD data.

As of October 2011, reliability growth plans called for the STOVL to have achieved at least 2.2 flying hours between failures and the CTOL at least 3.7 hours by this point in the program. The STOVL is significantly behind plans, achieving about 0.5 hours between failures, or less than 25 percent of the plan. CTOL variant has demonstrated 2.6 hours between failures, about 70 percent of the rate expected at this point in time. The carrier variant is slightly ahead of its plan; however, it has flown many fewer flights and hours than the other variants.

JSF officials said that reliability rates are tracking below expectations primarily because identified fixes to correct deficiencies are not being implemented and tested in a timely manner. Officials also said the growth rate is difficult to track and to confidently project expected performance at maturity because of insufficient data from the relatively small number of flight hours flown. Based on the initial low reliability demonstrated thus far, the Director of Operational Test and Evaluation reported that the JSF has a significant challenge ahead to provide sufficient reliability growth to meet the operational requirement.

Restructuring actions by the Department since early 2010 have provided the JSF program with more achievable development and production goals, and has reduced, but not eliminated, risks of additional retrofit costs due to concurrency in current and future lots. The Department has progressively lowered the production ramp-up rate and cut near term procurement quantities; fewer aircraft procured while testing is still ongoing lowers the risk of having to modify already produced aircraft. However, even with the most recent reductions in quantities, the program will still procure a large number of aircraft before system development is complete and flight testing confirms that the aircraft design and performance meets warfighter requirements. Table 4 shows the current plan that will procure 365 aircraft for $69 billion before the end of planned developmental flight tests.

Table 4: JSF Procurement Investments and Flight Test Progress

Fiscal years	2007	2008	2009	2010	2011	2012	2013	2014	2015	2016	2017
Cumulative procurement (billions of dollars)	$0.8	$3.5	$7.1	$14.3	$21.3	$27.6	$33.8	$40.1	$47.9	$57.8	$69.0
Cumulative aircraft procured	2	14	28	58	90	121	150	179	223	289	365
Percentage of total planned development flight tests completed (est.)	<1	<1	<1	1	5	17	32	52	72	91	100

Source: GAO analysis of DOD budget and test plan data.

Note: Advanced procurement funding from 2006 was incorporated into fiscal year 2007 total funding, as 2007 was the first year of aircraft procurement. Flight testing data reflect the percentage of the total flight test completed at the time of the planned investment decision, which is the beginning of the fiscal year.

Conclusions

The JSF remains the critical centerpiece of DOD's long-term tactical aircraft portfolio. System development of the aircraft and engine, ongoing for over a decade, continues to experience significant challenges. The program's strategic framework – laden with concurrency – has proved to be problematic and, ultimately, a very costly approach. DOD has lately acknowledged the undue risks from concurrency and accordingly reduced near-term procurement and devoted more time and resources to development and testing. These prudent actions have reduced, but not eliminated, concurrency risks of future cost growth from test discoveries driving changes to design and manufacturing processes. Substantial concurrency costs are expected to continue for several more years. Concurrency risks are not just limited to incurring extra modification costs, but ripple throughout the JSF program slowing aircraft deliveries, delaying release of software to testing, delaying pilot and maintainer training, and hindering the stand-up of base maintenance and supply activities, among other impacts.

Extensive restructuring actions over the last 2-plus years have placed the JSF program on a more achievable course, albeit a lengthier and more expensive one. At the same time, the near-constant churn, or change, in cost, schedule, and performance expectations has hampered oversight and insight into the program, in particular the ability to firmly assess progress and prospects for future success. The JSF program now needs to demonstrate that it can effectively perform against cost and schedule targets in the new baseline and deliver on its promises so that the warfighter can confidently establish basing plans, retire aging legacy aircraft, and acquire a support infrastructure. Addressing affordability risks will be critical in determining how many aircraft the U.S. and international partners can ultimately acquire and sustain over the life cycle. As currently structured, the program will require unprecedented levels of procurement funding during a period of more constrained defense budget expectations. Aircraft deferrals, risky funding assumptions, and future budget constraints make it prudent to evaluate potential impacts from reduced levels of funding. If funding demands cannot be fully met, it would be important for congressional and defense decisionmakers to understand the programmatic and cost impacts from lower levels of funding; however, DOD officials have not thoroughly analyzed JSF impacts should funding expectations be unmet. Going forward, it will be imperative to bring stability to the program and provide a firm understanding of near- and far-term financial requirements so that all parties—the Congress, Defense Department, and international partners—can reasonably project future budgets, set priorities, and make informed business-based decisions amid a tough fiscal environment.

Substantial cost overruns and delivery delays on the first four low rate initial production contracts indicate a need to improve inefficient manufacturing and supply processes before ramping up production to the rates expected. While some manufacturing and supply performance indicators are showing some improvements, parts shortages, supplier quality and performance problems, and manufacturing workarounds still need to be addressed. DOD's Independent Manufacturing Review Team identified global supply chain management as the most critical challenge for meeting production expectations. Effectively managing the expanding network of global suppliers and improving the supply chain will be key to improving cost and schedule outcomes, increasing manufacturing throughput, and enabling higher production rates.

Recommendations for Executive Action

Substantial quantities of JSF aircraft have been deferred to future years and funding requirements now average $12.5 billion through 2037. Aircraft deferrals, risky funding assumptions, and future budget constraints make it prudent to evaluate potential impacts from reduced levels of funding. Therefore, we recommend that the Secretary of Defense direct the Director of Cost Assessment and Program Evaluation perform an independent analysis of the impact lower annual funding levels would have on the program's cost and schedule. This sensitivity analysis should determine the impact of funding on aircraft deliveries, unit costs, and total tactical air force structure resulting from at least three different assumed annual funding profiles, all lower than the current funding projection.

Finally, because of the complexity and criticality of the global supply chain that has already experienced some problems, we recommend the Under Secretary of Defense for Acquisition, Technology and Logistics direct the JSF program office to conduct a comprehensive assessment of the supply chain and transportation network to ensure it is organized, secure, and capable of producing and delivering parts in the quantities and times needed to effectively and efficiently build and sustain over 3,000 aircraft for the U.S. and international partners. This assessment should summarize opportunities as well as challenges, augmenting and building upon the earlier efforts of the Independent Manufacturing Review Team and the recent sustainment study.

Agency Comments and our Evaluation

DOD provided us written comments on a draft of this report, which are reprinted in appendix II. DOD partially concurred with our first recommendation and fully concurred with our second. Officials also provided technical comments that we incorporated in the final report as appropriate.

DOD partially concurred with our recommendation to perform a sensitivity analysis of the impact lower annual funding levels would have on JSF cost and schedule and the total tactical air force structure. The Department stated that the Director of Cost Assessment and Program Evaluation regularly performs this kind of analysis as part of the annual budget review process. However, the Department's response emphasized that such analysis is pre-decisional and did not believe that sensitivity analyses based on notional funding levels should be published. We agree that this budget analysis has value and that it need not be published publicly; however, we believe its usefulness extends beyond the current budget period. Increasingly tough budget decisions amid a likely declining top-line defense budget are in the forecast, and this kind of sensitivity analysis of the impact of potential lower funding levels could better inform defense leadership and the Congress on the longer-term impacts on JSF program outcomes and force structure implications.

DOD concurred with our recommendation to comprehensively assess the global supply chain and transportation network. The written response indicated that annual production readiness reviews undertaken by the contractor and JSF program office were sufficient and better structured to manage issues over several years than a one time, large scale study. We agree that annual targeted reviews are important and conducive to good near-term management, but continue to believe that these should be supplemented by a longer-term and more forward-looking study as we have recommended along the lines of the Independent Manufacturing Review Team.

We are sending copies of this report to the Secretary of Defense; the Secretaries of the Air Force, Army, and Navy; and the Director of the Office of Management and Budget. The report also is available at no charge on the GAO Web site at http://www.gao.gov.

If you or your staff have any questions concerning this report, please contact me at (202) 512-4841 or sullivanm@gao.gov. Contact points for our Offices of Congressional Relations and Public Affairs may be found on the last page of this report. Staff members making key contributions to this report are listed in Appendix VI.

Michael J. Sullivan
Director
Acquisition and Sourcing Management

List of Committees

The Honorable Carl Levin
Chairman
The Honorable John McCain
Ranking Member
Committee on Armed Services
United States Senate

The Honorable Daniel K. Inouye
Chairman
The Honorable Thad Cochran
Ranking Member
Subcommittee on Defense
Committee on Appropriations
United States Senate

The Honorable Howard P. McKeon
Chairman
The Honorable Adam Smith
Ranking Member
Committee on Armed Services
House of Representatives

The Honorable C.W. Bill Young
Chairman
The Honorable Norman D. Dicks
Ranking Member
Subcommittee on Defense
Committee on Appropriations
House of Representatives

Appendix I: Scope and Methodology

To determine the Joint Strike Fighter (JSF) program's progress in meeting cost, schedule, and performance goals, we received briefings by program and contractor officials and reviewed financial management reports, budget documents, annual Selected Acquisition Reports, monthly status reports, performance indicators, and other data. We identified changes in cost and schedule, and obtained officials' reasons for these changes. We interviewed officials from the JSF program, contractors, and the Department of Defense (DOD) to obtain their views on progress, ongoing concerns and actions taken to address them, and future plans to complete JSF development and accelerate procurement. At the time of our review, the most recent Selected Acquisition Report available was dated December 31, 2011. Throughout most of our review, DOD was in the process of preparing the new acquisition program baseline, issued in March 2012, which reflected updated cost and schedule projections.

In assessing program cost estimates, we evaluated program cost estimates in the Selected Acquisition Reports since the program's inception, reviewed the recent independent cost estimate completed by DOD's Cost Analysis and Program Evaluation (CAPE), and analyzed fiscal year President's Budget data. We interviewed JSF program office officials, members of CAPE, prime and engine contractors, and Defense Contract Management Agency officials to understand methodology, data, and approach in developing cost estimates and monitoring cost performance.

To assess plans, progress, and risks in test activities, we examined program documents and interviewed DOD, program office, and contractor officials about current test plans and progress. To assess progress toward test plans, we compared the number of test points accomplished as of December 2011 to the program's 2011 plan for test point progress. We also discussed related software development, test, and integration with Defense Contract Management Agency (DCMA) and Director, Operational Test, and Evaluation (DOT&E) officials and reviewed DOT&E annual assessments of the JSF program, the Joint Strike Fighter Operational Test Team Report, and the F-35 Joint Strike Fighter Concurrency Quick Look Review.

To assess the program's plans and risk in manufacturing and its capacity to accelerate production, we analyzed manufacturing cost and work performance data to assess progress against plans. We reviewed data and briefings provided by the program and DCMA to assess supplier performance and ability to support accelerated production in the near term. We also determined reasons for manufacturing delays, discussed program and contractor plans to improve, and projected the impact on development and operational tests. We interviewed contractor and DCMA officials to discuss the Earned Value Management System but did not conduct any analysis since the system has not yet been re-validated by DCMA.

In performing our work, we obtained information and interviewed officials from the JSF Joint Program Office, Arlington, Virginia; Defense Contract Management Agency, Fort Worth, Texas; Lockheed Martin Aeronautics, Fort Worth, Texas; Defense Contract Management Agency, East Hartford, Connecticut; and Pratt & Whitney, Middletown, Connecticut. We also met with and obtained data from the following offices from the Secretary of Defense in Washington, D.C.: Director, Operational Test and Evaluation; Cost Assessment and Program Evaluation; and Systems Engineering.

To assess the reliability of DOD and contractor data we reviewed the sources and uses of the data, evaluated existing information about the data, and interviewed agency officials knowledgeable about the data. We determined that the data were sufficiently reliable for the purposes of this report. We conducted this performance audit from June 2011 to June 2012 in accordance with generally accepted government auditing standards. Those standards require that we plan and perform the audit to obtain sufficient, appropriate evidence to provide a reasonable basis for our findings and conclusions based on our audit objectives. We believe that the evidence obtained provides a reasonable basis for our findings and conclusions based on our audit objectives.

Appendix II: Comments from the Department of Defense

OFFICE OF THE UNDER SECRETARY OF DEFENSE
3000 DEFENSE PENTAGON
WASHINGTON, DC 20301-3000

ACQUISITION,
TECHNOLOGY
AND LOGISTICS

JUN 11 2012

Mr. Michael Sullivan
Director, Acquisition and Sourcing Management
U.S. Government Accountability Office
441 G Street, N.W.
Washington, DC 20548

Dear Mr. Sullivan:

This is the Department of Defense (DoD) response to the GAO draft report, GAO-12-437, "JOINT STRIKE FIGHTER: DoD Actions Needed to Further Enhance Restructuring and Address Affordability Risks," dated May 1, 2012 (GAO Code 120995). Detailed comments on the report recommendations are enclosed.

The DoD partially concurs with the first recommendation and concurs with the second recommendation. The rationale and actions taken by the DoD are included in the enclosure.

We appreciate the opportunity to comment on the draft report. My point of contact for this effort is Lt Col Amy McCain, 703-697-2573, Amy.McCain@osd.mil.

Sincerely,

David G. Ahern
Deputy Assistant Secretary of Defense
Strategic and Tactical Systems

Enclosure:
As stated

GAO DRAFT REPORT DATED MAY 1, 2012
GAO-12-437 (GAO CODE 120995)

"JOINT STRIKE FIGHTER: DOD ACTIONS NEEDED TO FURTHER
ENHANCE RESTRUCTURING AND ADDRESS
AFFORDABILITY RISKS"

The Department remains committed to the F-35 Joint Strike Fighter (JSF)
program as the backbone of the future tactical aircraft inventory for the Air Force,
Navy, Marine Corps, as well as our International Partners. The Fiscal Year (FY)
2013 President's Budget (PB) demonstrates this commitment to the F-35 with $9.3
billion for continued system development, test and procurement.

The F-35 development program has been replanned and is now resourced
with realistic planning factors to complete the required Block 3 capability testing
by the end of 2016. In March 2012, the program completed the Milestone B
recertification and established the new acquisition program baseline. Production
rates were held to 29 per year through 2014 to reduce concurrency risk and permit
additional progress on the test program before increasing production. The
Department is committed to delivering F-35 aircraft that meet the Services'
requirements, in addition to controlling and reducing costs wherever and whenever
possible, to provide the Services an affordable tactical aviation capability.

DEPARTMENT OF DEFENSE COMMENTS
TO THE GAO RECOMMENDATIONS

RECOMMENDATION 1: The GAO recommends that the Secretary of Defense
direct the Director of Cost Assessment and Program Evaluation (CAPE) perform
an independent analysis of the impact lower annual funding levels would have on
the program's cost and schedule. This sensitivity analysis should determine the
impact of funding on aircraft deliveries, unit costs, and total tactical air force
structure resulting from at least 3 different assumed annual funding profiles, all
lower than the current funding projection.

DoD RESPONSE: Partially Concur. The Department agrees that there is value
in examining the sensitivity of the costs of JSF procurement against varying levels
of procurement funding. In fact, CAPE regularly performs this type of analysis as
a part of the deliberative, pre-decisional, program/budget review process that
culminates in the submission of the annual President's Budget request for DoD.
For example, during the Department's preparation of the budget submission for

2

Fiscal Year (FY) 2013, CAPE developed analyses involving several alternative F-35 procurement profiles for consideration by the senior Department leadership. The analysis included different U.S. and international partner annual F-35 procurement quantities during FY 2013-17.

Given the interrelationships of F-35 programmatic costs, this type of analysis should not be done in isolation. It is important that the analysis consider a broader context, including the effect of the procurement profiles on the industrial base, legacy fleet operations, and international partner participation. The Department does not believe there is value in publishing sensitivity analyses for F-35 based on notionally-defined funding levels. As has always been the case, CAPE will continue to conduct analyses of alternative annual procurement profiles to support pre-decisional deliberations within the Department.

RECOMMENDATION 2: The GAO recommends that the Under Secretary of Defense for Acquisition, Technology and Logistics direct the JSF program office to conduct a comprehensive assessment of the supply chain and transportation network to ensure it is organized, secure, and capable of producing and delivering parts in the quantities and times needed to effectively and efficiently build and sustain over 3,000 aircraft for the U.S. and international partners. This assessment should summarize opportunities as well as challenges, augmenting and building upon the earlier efforts of the Independent Manufacturing Review Team and the recent sustainment study.

DoD RESPONSE: Concur. The Department agrees that there is value in a comprehensive assessment to identify opportunities and challenges of the supply chain and transportation network. However, the Department does not agree with directing the program office to begin a separate and additional effort. Currently, Lockheed Martin and the Joint Program Office conduct annual Production Readiness Reviews (PRR) that assess the capabilities and risks in the supply chain to support the production ramp and sustain the fleet. The Department believes that the annual review is more flexible and more applicable to the overall management of the program, and is better structured to maintain long-term visibility to manage issues over several years, than a one time, large scale study.

Appendix III: Prior GAO Reports and DOD Responses

GAO report	Est. dev. costs dev. length aircraft unit cost	Key program event	Primary GAO message	DOD response and actions
2001 GAO-02-39	$34.4 Billion 10 years $69 Million	Start of system development and demonstration approved.	Critical technologies needed for key aircraft performance elements not mature. Program should delay start of system development until critical technologies mature to acceptable levels.	DOD did not delay start of system development and demonstration stating technologies were at acceptable maturity levels and will manage risks in development.
2005 GAO-05-271	$44.8 Billion 12 years $82 Million	The program undergoes re-plan to address higher than expected design weight, which added $7 billion and 18 months to development schedule.	We recommended that the program reduce risks and establish executable business case that is knowledge-based with an evolutionary acquisition strategy.	DOD partially concurred but did not adjust strategy, believing that its approach is balanced between cost, schedule and technical risk.
2006 GAO-06-356	$45.7 Billion 12 years $86 Million	Program sets in motion plan to enter production in 2007 shortly after first flight of the non-production representative aircraft.	The program plans to enter production with less than 1 percent of testing complete. We recommended program delay investing in production until flight testing shows that JSF performs as expected.	DOD partially concurred but did not delay start of production because it believed the risk level was appropriate.
2007 GAO-07-360	$44.5 Billion 12 years $104 Million	Congress reduced funding for first two low-rate production buys thereby slowing the ramp up of production.	Progress was being made but concerns remained about undue overlap in testing and production. We recommended limits to annual production quantities to 24 a year until flying quantities are demonstrated.	DOD non-concurred and felt that the program had an acceptable level of concurrency and an appropriate acquisition strategy.
2008 GAO-08-388	$44.2 Billion 12 years $104 Million	DOD implemented a Mid-Course Risk Reduction Plan to replenish management reserves from about $400 million to about $1 billion by reducing test resources.	We believed new plan actually increased risks and recommended that DOD revise the plan to address concerns about testing, use of management reserves, and manufacturing. We determined that the cost estimate was not reliable and that a new cost estimate and schedule risk assessment is needed.	DOD did not revise risk plan or restore testing resources, stating that it will monitor the new plan and adjust it if necessary. Consistent with a report recommendation, a new cost estimate was eventually prepared, but DOD refused to do a risk and uncertainty analysis that we felt was important to provide a range estimate of potential outcomes.

GAO report	Est. dev. costs dev. length aircraft unit cost	Key program event	Primary GAO message	DOD response and actions
2009 GAO-09-303	$44.4 Billion 13 years $104 Million	The program increased the cost estimate and adds a year to development but accelerated the production ramp up. Independent DOD cost estimate (JET I) projects even higher costs and further delays.	Because of development problems, we stated that moving forward with an accelerated procurement plan and use of cost reimbursement contracts is very risky. We recommended the program report on the risks and mitigation strategy for this approach.	DOD agreed to report its contracting strategy and plans to Congress. In response to our report recommendation, DOD subsequently agreed to do a schedule risk analysis. The program reported completing the first schedule risk assessment in summer 2011 with plans to update about every 6 months. In February 2010, the Department announced a major restructuring of the JSF program, including reduced procurement and a planned move to fixed-price contracts.
2010 GAO-10-382	$49.3 Billion 15 years $112 Million	The program was restructured to reflect findings of recent independent cost team (JET II) and independent manufacturing review team. As a result, development funds increased, test aircraft were added, the schedule was extended, and the early production rate decreased.	Because of additional costs and schedule delays, the program's ability to meet warfighter requirements on time is at risk. We recommend the program complete a full comprehensive cost estimate and assess warfighter and IOC requirements. We suggest that Congress require DOD to prepare a "system maturity matrix"–a tool for tying annual procurement requests to demonstrated progress.	DOD continued restructuring actions and announced plans to increase test resources and lower the production rate. Independent review teams evaluated aircraft and engine manufacturing processes. As we projected in this report, cost increases later resulted in a Nunn-McCurdy breach. Military services are currently reviewing capability requirements as we recommended.
2011 GAO-11-325	$51.8 Billion 16 years $133 Million	Restructuring continued following the Nunn-McCurdy certification with additional development cost increases; schedule growth; further reduction in near-term procurement quantities; and decreased the rate of increase for future production. The Secretary of Defense placed the STOVL variant on a 2 year probation; decoupled STOVL from the other variants in the testing program because of lingering technical issues; and reduced STOVL production plans for fiscal years 2011 to 2013.	The restructuring actions are positive and if implemented properly, should lead to more achievable and predictable outcomes. Concurrency of development, test, and production is substantial and provides risk to the program. We recommended the program maintain funding levels as budgeted in the FY 2012-2016 future years' defense plan; establish criteria for STOVL probation; and conduct an independent review of software development, integration, and test processes.	DOD concurred with all three of the recommendations. In January 2012, the Secretary of Defense lifted STOVL probation, citing improved performance. Subsequently, the Secretary further reduced procurement quantities, decreasing funding requirements through 2016. The initial independent software assessment began in September 2011, and ongoing reviews are planned through 2012.

Source: DOD data and GAO analysis in prior reports cited above.

Appendix IV: Budgeted Funding and Procurement Quantities, FY 2011-2017

(Dollars in millions)

Development funding	2011	2012	2013	2014	2015	2016	2017	Total
Air Force (CTOL)	$932	$1,398	$1,218	$1,069	$741	$520	$386	$6,263
Navy (CV)	654	659	744	702	584	458	350	4,151
Marine Corps (STOVL)	602	652	737	693	575	448	340	4,048
U.S. total	**$2,188**	**$2,708**	**$2,699**	**$2,465**	**$1,900**	**$1,427**	**$1,075**	**$14,462**

Procurement funding	2011	2012	2013	2014	2015	2016	2017	Total
Air Force (CTOL)	$4,302	$3,519	$3,566	$3,515	$4,793	$6,250	$6,202	$32,146
Navy (CV)	1,853	1,557	1,073	1,274	1,432	1,724	2,430	11,343
Marine Corps (STOVL)	838	1,259	1,511	1,521	1,562	1,953	2,577	11,221
U.S. total	**$6,993**	**$6,335**	**$6,149**	**$6,311**	**$7,787**	**$9,927**	**$11,208**	**$54,710**

Quantity	2011	2012	2013	2014	2015	2016	2017	Total
Air Force (CTOL)	22	18	19	19	32	48	48	206
Navy (CV)	7	7	4	4	6	9	14	51
Marine Corps (STOVL)	3	6	6	6	6	9	14	50
U.S. total	**32**	**31**	**29**	**29**	**44**	**66**	**76**	**307**

Source: GAO analysis of Fiscal Year 2013 President's Budget materials and JSF program office data.

Note: Numbers may not add due to rounding.

Appendix V: Short Takeoff and Vertical Landing Aircraft Probation Period and Progress

In January 2011, the Secretary of Defense placed the short takeoff and vertical landing (STOVL) aircraft on "probation" for 2 years, citing technical issues unique to the variant that would add to the aircraft's cost and weight. The probation limited the U.S. STOVL procurement to three aircraft in fiscal year 2011 and six aircraft in fiscal year 2012 and decoupled STOVL testing from CV and CTOL testing so as not to delay those variants. The 2 year probation was expected to provide enough time to address STOVL-specific technical issues, engineer solutions, and assess their impact. It was presumed that at the end of probation, an informed decision could be made about whether and how to proceed with STOVL, but no specific exit criteria were established. In our 2011 report[1], we recommended that the program establish criteria for the STOVL probation period and take additional steps to sustain individual attention on STOVL-specific issues to ensure cost and schedule milestones were achieved in order to deliver required warfighter capabilities.

In January 2012, the new Secretary of Defense lifted the STOVL probation after 1 year, citing improved performance and completion of the initial sea trials aboard the U.S.S. Wasp as a basis for the decision. In its report to Congress[2], the Department explained that STOVL progress was continually monitored throughout the probation period with a holistic view of the weapon system, and reiterated that the STOVL was not placed on probation with specific exit criteria. The report stated that the Commandant of the Marine Corps completed monthly reviews of STOVL progress in addition to the monthly Service Acquisition Executive reviews of the JSF program, and that this provided the individual focus required to balance cost, schedule, and development progress against warfighter utility. These reviews assessed categories of STOVL weight and vertical lift propulsion performance, availability, and ship suitability in fleet operation, as well as the costs to modify, operate and procure the aircraft. Throughout 2011, the STOVL variant increased test flight rates and STOVL-specific mode testing, surpassing planned test point progress for the year. In ending probation, the Department concluded that sufficient progress in STOVL development, test, and production had been made such that no uniquely distinguishing issues required that it receive more

---

[1] GAO-11-325.

[2] Under Secretary of Defense Acquisition, Technology and Logistics Report to Congress on Probationary Period in Development of Short Take-off, Vertical Landing Variant of the Joint Strike Fighter: National Defense Authorization Act for Fiscal Year 2012, section 148.

scrutiny than the other two variants. According to the department, interim solutions are in place to mitigate the lingering technical issues with the STOVL and permanent solutions are in varying stages of development or implementation.

While the probation period did not include specific criteria, the reasons given for probation were to address technical issues, engineer solutions, and assess impact, and it was expected to take 2 years to do so. Although we note that several technical issues have been addressed and some potential solutions engineered, assessing whether the deficiencies are resolved is ongoing and, in some cases, will not be known for years. Table 5 provides details on the STOVL technical problems identified at the onset of probation, the efforts to resolve the problems, and timeframes for implementing fixes. According to the program, of the five specific problems cited, two are considered to be fixed (bulkhead cracks and air inlet door loads) while the other three have temporary fixes in place. The Director, Operational Test and Evaluation (DOT&E) officials reported that significant work remains to verify and incorporate modifications to correct known STOVL deficiencies and prepare the system for operational use. Until the proposed technical solutions have been fully tested and demonstrated, it cannot be determined if the technical problems have been resolved.

Table 5: STOVL Technical Problems Identified for Probation Period

Technical Problem	Design Fix	Reported Status	Production Cut-in
Bulkhead cracks developed before 2,000 hours of fatigue/durability testing. Requirement is 8,000 hours.	Bulkhead redesign for production, with fixes identified for retrofit as needed.	Redesign has been completed and fatigue/durability test resumed in January 2012.	-
Excessive loads on the auxiliary air inlet doors, causing higher than expected wear and fatigue.	Door redesign.	Flight testing began in December 2011 on redesigned door installed on BF-1. According to the program office, analyses of the results from early test flights are promising.	BF-38 LRIP 6
Higher-than-expected heating of the lift fan clutch during conventional flight.	An interim solution is a temperature sensor that alerts the pilot to take corrective action if the clutch exceeds acceptable temperatures. A final solution for the heat problem has yet to be determined.	The temperature sensor has been added to aircraft as the interim measure. A detailed root cause investigation for a permanent fix to eliminate lift fan clutch heating is underway.	BF-44 LRIP 7
Thermal growth of the airframe and engine exceed the current lift fan drive shaft stretch/compression capability.	Interim solution is to add spacers to the lift fan driveshaft to accommodate unanticipated thermal expansion and contraction. This eliminates airworthiness concerns. Final solution is to redesign the driveshaft.	Spacers have been added to ensure airworthiness for the interim solution. A new driveshaft that can meet actual aircraft environmental requirements is in the early phases of the design process.	BF-44 LRIP 7
Roll post nozzle bay temperatures exceed current actuator capability.	Interim solution is to insulate the actuator with a thermal blanket. Final fix expected to be a redesigned actuator.	Airworthiness risk mitigated by thermal blanket. The critical design review for a new actuator design that will eliminate the need for a thermal blanket was conducted January 2012.	TBD

Source: GAO analysis of DOD data.

Appendix VI: GAO Contact and Staff Acknowledgments

GAO Contact	Michael Sullivan (202) 512-4841 or sullivanm@gao.gov
Acknowledgments	In addition to the contact name above, the following staff members made key contributions to this report: Bruce Fairbairn, Assistant Director; Charlie Shivers; Sean Merrill; LeAnna Parkey; Dr. W. Kendal Roberts; Laura Greifner; and Matt Lea.

Related GAO Products

Defense Acquisitions: Assessments of Selected Weapon Programs. GAO-12-400SP. Washington, D.C.: March 29, 2012.

Joint Strike Fighter: Restructuring Added Resources and Reduced Risk, but Concurrency Is Still a Major Concern. GAO-12-525T. Washington, D.C.: March 20, 2012.

Joint Strike Fighter: Implications of Program Restructuring and Other Recent Developments on Key Aspects of DOD's Prior Alternate Engine Analyses. GAO-11-903R. Washington, D.C.: September 14, 2011.

Joint Strike Fighter: Restructuring Places Program on Firmer Footing, but Progress Is Still Lagging. GAO-11-677T. Washington, D.C.: May 19, 2011.

Joint Strike Fighter: Restructuring Places Program on Firmer Footing, but Progress Still Lags. GAO-11-325. Washington, D.C.: April 7, 2011.

Joint Strike Fighter: Restructuring Should Improve Outcomes, but Progress Is Still Lagging Overall. GAO-11-450T. Washington, D.C.: March 15, 2011.

Tactical Aircraft: Air Force Fighter Force Structure Reports Generally Addressed Congressional Mandates, but Reflected Dated Plans and Guidance, and Limited Analyses. GAO-11-323R. Washington, D.C.: February 24, 2011.

Defense Management: DOD Needs to Monitor and Assess Corrective Actions Resulting from Its Corrosion Study of the F-35 Joint Strike Fighter. GAO-11-171R. Washington D.C.: December 16, 2010.

Joint Strike Fighter: Assessment of DOD's Funding Projection for the F136 Alternate Engine. GAO-10-1020R. Washington, D.C.: September 15, 2010.

Tactical Aircraft: DOD's Ability to Meet Future Requirements is Uncertain, with Key Analyses Needed to Inform Upcoming Investment Decisions. GAO-10-789. Washington, D.C.: July 29, 2010.

Defense Acquisitions: Assessments of Selected Weapon Programs. GAO-10-388SP. Washington, D.C.: March 30, 2010.

Joint Strike Fighter: Significant Challenges and Decisions Ahead. GAO-10-478T. Washington, D.C.: March 24, 2010.

Joint Strike Fighter: Additional Costs and Delays Risk Not Meeting Warfighter Requirements on Time. GAO-10-382. Washington, D.C.: March 19, 2010.

Joint Strike Fighter: Significant Challenges Remain as DOD Restructures Program. GAO-10-520T. Washington, D.C.: March 11, 2010.

Joint Strike Fighter: Strong Risk Management Essential as Program Enters Most Challenging Phase. GAO-09-711T. Washington, D.C.: May 20, 2009.

Defense Acquisitions: Assessments of Selected Weapon Programs. GAO-09-326SP. Washington, D.C.: March 30, 2009.

Joint Strike Fighter: Accelerating Procurement before Completing Development Increases the Government's Financial Risk. GAO-09-303. Washington D.C.: March 12, 2009.

Defense Acquisitions: Better Weapon Program Outcomes Require Discipline, Accountability, and Fundamental Changes in the Acquisition Environment. GAO-08-782T. Washington, D.C.: June 3, 2008.

Defense Acquisitions: Assessments of Selected Weapon Programs. GAO-08-467SP. Washington, D.C.: March 31, 2008.

Joint Strike Fighter: Impact of Recent Decisions on Program Risks. GAO-08-569T. Washington, D.C.: March 11, 2008.

Joint Strike Fighter: Recent Decisions by DOD Add to Program Risks. GAO-08-388. Washington, D.C.: March 11, 2008.

Tactical Aircraft: DOD Needs a Joint and Integrated Investment Strategy. GAO-07-415. Washington, D.C.: April 2, 2007.

Defense Acquisitions: Analysis of Costs for the Joint Strike Fighter Engine Program. GAO-07-656T. Washington, D.C.: March 22, 2007.

Joint Strike Fighter: Progress Made and Challenges Remain. GAO-07-360. Washington, D.C.: March 15, 2007.

Tactical Aircraft: DOD's Cancellation of the Joint Strike Fighter Alternate Engine Program Was Not Based on a Comprehensive Analysis. GAO-06-717R. Washington, D.C.: May 22, 2006.

Defense Acquisitions: Major Weapon Systems Continue to Experience Cost and Schedule Problems under DOD's Revised Policy. GAO-06-368. Washington, D.C.: April 13, 2006.

Defense Acquisitions: Actions Needed to Get Better Results on Weapons Systems Investments. GAO-06-585T. Washington, D.C.: April 5, 2006.

Tactical Aircraft: Recapitalization Goals Are Not Supported by Knowledge-Based F-22A and JSF Business Cases. GAO-06-487T. Washington, D.C.: March 16, 2006.

Joint Strike Fighter: DOD Plans to Enter Production before Testing Demonstrates Acceptable Performance. GAO-06-356. Washington, D.C.: March 15, 2006.

Joint Strike Fighter: Management of the Technology Transfer Process. GAO-06-364. Washington, D.C.: March 14, 2006.

Tactical Aircraft: F/A-22 and JSF Acquisition Plans and Implications for Tactical Aircraft Modernization. GAO-05-519T. Washington, D.C: April 6, 2005.

Tactical Aircraft: Opportunity to Reduce Risks in the Joint Strike Fighter Program with Different Acquisition Strategy. GAO-05-271. Washington, D.C.: March 15, 2005.

GAO's Mission	The Government Accountability Office, the audit, evaluation, and investigative arm of Congress, exists to support Congress in meeting its constitutional responsibilities and to help improve the performance and accountability of the federal government for the American people. GAO examines the use of public funds; evaluates federal programs and policies; and provides analyses, recommendations, and other assistance to help Congress make informed oversight, policy, and funding decisions. GAO's commitment to good government is reflected in its core values of accountability, integrity, and reliability.
Obtaining Copies of GAO Reports and Testimony	The fastest and easiest way to obtain copies of GAO documents at no cost is through GAO's website (www.gao.gov). Each weekday afternoon, GAO posts on its website newly released reports, testimony, and correspondence. To have GAO e-mail you a list of newly posted products, go to www.gao.gov and select "E-mail Updates."
Order by Phone	The price of each GAO publication reflects GAO's actual cost of production and distribution and depends on the number of pages in the publication and whether the publication is printed in color or black and white. Pricing and ordering information is posted on GAO's website, http://www.gao.gov/ordering.htm.
	Place orders by calling (202) 512-6000, toll free (866) 801-7077, or TDD (202) 512-2537.
	Orders may be paid for using American Express, Discover Card, MasterCard, Visa, check, or money order. Call for additional information.
Connect with GAO	Connect with GAO on Facebook, Flickr, Twitter, and YouTube. Subscribe to our RSS Feeds or E-mail Updates. Listen to our Podcasts. Visit GAO on the web at www.gao.gov.
To Report Fraud, Waste, and Abuse in Federal Programs	Contact: Website: www.gao.gov/fraudnet/fraudnet.htm E-mail: fraudnet@gao.gov Automated answering system: (800) 424-5454 or (202) 512-7470
Congressional Relations	Katherine Siggerud, Managing Director, siggerudk@gao.gov, (202) 512-4400, U.S. Government Accountability Office, 441 G Street NW, Room 7125, Washington, DC 20548
Public Affairs	Chuck Young, Managing Director, youngc1@gao.gov, (202) 512-4800 U.S. Government Accountability Office, 441 G Street NW, Room 7149 Washington, DC 20548